AMERICA ★ THE ★ BEAUTIFUL

How to Use This Book

Look for these special features in this book:

SIDEBARS, **CHARTS**, **GRAPHS**, and original **MAPS** expand your understanding of what's being discussed—and also make useful sources for classroom reports.

FAQs answer common **F**requently **A**sked **Q**uestions about people, places, and things.

WOW FACTORS offer "Who knew?" facts to keep you thinking.

TRAVEL GUIDE gives you tips on exploring the state—either in person or right from your chair!

PROJECT ROOM provides fun ideas for school assignments and incredible research projects. Plus, there's a guide to primary sources—what they are and how to cite them.

Please note: All statistics are as up-to-date as possible at the time of publication. Population data is taken from the 2010 census.

Consultants: Pabby Arnold, Head of Children's Services, East Baton Rouge Parish Library; Paul V. Heinrich, Louisiana Geological Survey, Louisiana State University; William Loren Katz

Book production by The Design Lab

Library of Congress Cataloging-in-Publication Data
Lassieur, Allison.
Louisiana / by Allison Lassieur. — Revised Edition.
pages cm. — (America the beautiful. Third series)
Includes bibliographical references and index.
ISBN 978-0-531-24886-7 (lib. bdg.)
1. Louisiana—Juvenile literature. I. Title.
F369.3.L37 2014
976.3—dc23   2013032186

©2014, 2008 Scholastic Inc.
All rights reserved. Published in 2014 by Children's Press, an imprint of Scholastic Inc.
Printed in the United States of America 141
SCHOLASTIC, CHILDREN'S PRESS, and associated logos are trademarks and/or registered trademarks of Scholastic Inc.

1 2 3 4 5 6 7 8 9 10 R 23 22 21 20 19 18 17 16 15 14

Louisiana

BY ALLISON LASSIEUR

Third Series, Revised Edition

Children's Press®
An Imprint of Scholastic Inc.
New York ★ Toronto ★ London ★ Auckland ★ Sydney
Mexico City ★ New Delhi ★ Hong Kong
Danbury, Connecticut

CONTENTS

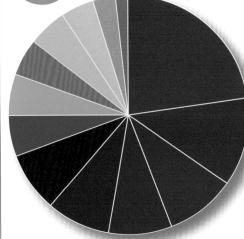

4 GROWTH AND CHANGE

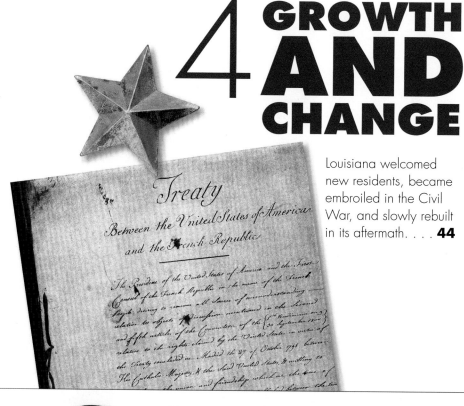

Louisiana welcomed new residents, became embroiled in the Civil War, and slowly rebuilt in its aftermath. . . . **44**

MORE MODERN TIMES

The state perseveres through the challenges of world wars, the civil rights movement, and a devastating hurricane. . . **58**

5

9 TRAVEL GUIDE

Take a boat tour of the Atchafalaya Swamp. Sway to jazz music. Chow down on mouthwatering Cajun food. **108**

PROJECT ROOM

★

ARKANSAS

SHREVEPORT

MONROE

Poverty Point
National
Monument

Driskill
Mountain

Toledo
Bend
Reservoir

Red

Black

Mississippi

N
W E
S

MISSISSIPPI

NATCHITOCHES

Kisatchie
National
Forest

KISATCHIE
National
Forest

0   60
Miles

ALEXANDRIA

LOUISIANA

Old State
Capitol
Museum

TEXAS

Calcasieu

Atchafalaya

Bourbon

The Causeway

Lake
Pontchartrain

Sabine

The Cajun
Prairie

Evangeline Oak Tree

SLIDELL

LAKE CHARLES

Frog
Festival

BATON ROUGE

Historic
French
Quarter

NEW ORLEANS

Mardi Gras
Festival

LAFAYETTE

Intracoastal

Waterway

Jazz
Fest

Mississippi

Atchafalaya
Swamp

Atchafalaya
Bay

Gulf of
Mexico

Mississippi
River and
Delta

GULF OF MEXICO

QUICK FACTS

State capital: Baton Rouge
Largest city: New Orleans
Total area: 51,840 square miles
(134,265 sq km)
Highest point: Driskill Mountain,
535 feet (163 m)
Lowest point: –8 feet (–2.4 m) at
New Orleans

ALABAMA

GEORGIA

Welcome to Louisiana!

HOW DID LOUISIANA GET ITS NAME?

In 1682, a Frenchman named René-Robert Cavelier, Sieur de La Salle, put together an expedition and journeyed south from Canada, hoping to get rich in the fur trade. By early April, La Salle and his group arrived at the mouth of the mighty Mississippi and claimed all the lands for France. La Salle named the territory Louisiana, in honor of France's king, Louis XIV. This territory eventually became the state of Louisiana.

LOUISIANA

FLORIDA

GULF OF MEXICO

READ ABOUT

A white heron guards her two chicks.

LAND

★

FROM ITS HIGHEST POINT OF 535 FEET (163 METERS) ATOP DRISKILL MOUNTAIN TO ITS LOWEST POINT OF 8 FEET (2.4 M) BELOW SEA LEVEL IN NEW ORLEANS, LOUISIANA IS ONE WET STATE. Thousands of rivers, lakes, streams, swamps, and marshlands mark its 51,840 square miles (134,265 square kilometers). The mightiest waterway in Louisiana is the Mississippi River, which flows through the state and empties billions of gallons of water into the Gulf of Mexico.

GETTING TO KNOW LOUISIANA

Wetlands, including vast swamps and huge bayous, cover Louisiana—more than 7 million acres (2.8 million hectares) of them. Water is such a part of Louisiana life that some of its nicknames, such as "Bayou State" and "Child of the Mississippi," celebrate Louisiana's many rivers and waterways.

Louisiana Topography

Use the color-coded elevation chart to see on the map Louisiana's high points (yellow and orange) and low points (green to dark green). Elevation is measured as the distance above or below sea level.

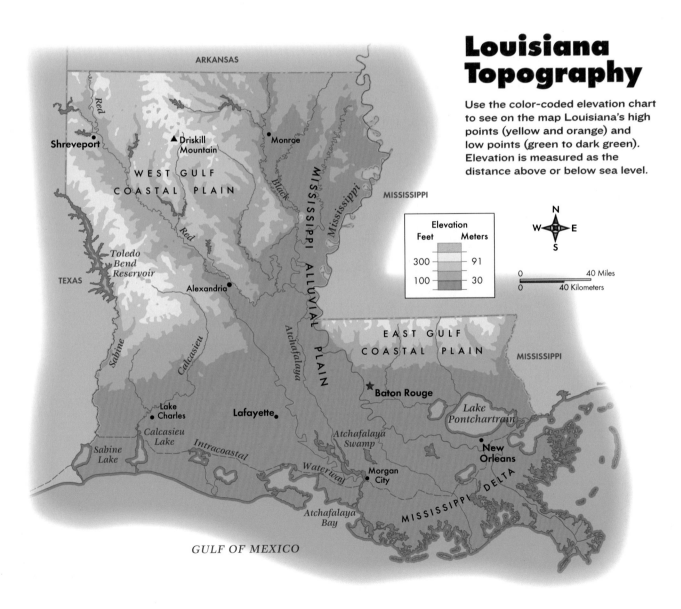

Elevation	
Feet	Meters
300	91
100	30

This is an aerial view of Madisonville and Lake Pontchartrain.

You'll find more than swamps and wetlands in the state. Rolling hills, grass prairies, and forests cover parts of Louisiana. What it doesn't have, though, are mountain ranges. Louisiana is a very low-lying state. In fact, at the lowest points near the coast, the land is 8 feet (2.4 m) below sea level.

The Gulf of Mexico stretches along Louisiana's southern border. Texas borders Louisiana to the west, while Arkansas lies to the north, and Mississippi sits to the east.

Louisiana Geo-Facts

This chart shows Louisiana's geographical highlights and the rank of the state's total area, land area, and water area compared with all 50 states.

Total area; rank . . . . 51,840 square miles (134,265 sq km); 31st
Land; rank . . . . .43,562 square miles (112,825 sq km); 33rd
Water; rank . . . . 8,278 square miles (21,440 sq km); 5th
   Inland water; rank . . . . 4,154 square miles (10,759 sq km); 5th
   Coastal water; rank . . . . . . .1,935 square miles (5,012 sq km); 3rd
   Territorial water; rank . . . . . 2,189 square miles (5,669 sq km); 5th
Geographic center . . . . .Avoyelles, 3 miles (5 km) southeast of Marksville
Latitude . . . . 28° 00′ N to 33° 00′ N
Longitude . . . . 89° 00′ W to 94° 00′ W
Highest point . . . . .Driskill Mountain, 535 feet (163 m)
Lowest point . . . . −8 feet (−2.4 m) at New Orleans
Largest city . . . . New Orleans
Longest river . . . . Mississippi River, 305 miles (491 km) in Louisiana
of a total length of 2,348 miles (3,779 km)

Source: U.S. Census Bureau, 2010 census

The state of Rhode Island would fit inside Louisiana more than 33 times!

Rivers, streams, and other waterways can cause erosion. As the soil wears away, the result can be land formations such as this one, Marchive's Bluff, in Tunica Hills.

Q8 WHAT IS THE DIFFERENCE BETWEEN A SWAMP AND A BAYOU?

A8 A bayou is a slow-moving stream that's bigger than a creek but smaller than a river. A swamp is a large, low-lying flooded area. Swamps usually include sections of forests or small islands.

WORD TO KNOW

hardwood *a tree that sheds its leaves at the end of the growing season*

LAND REGIONS

Louisiana is split roughly from north to south into three land regions: the East Gulf Coastal Plain, the Mississippi Alluvial Plain, and the West Gulf Coastal Plain. Each one has its own unique landforms, plants, and animals.

East Gulf Coastal Plain

If you look at a map, Louisiana is shaped like a boot. The East Gulf Coastal Plain is in the "toe" part of the boot, which includes the land east of the Mississippi River and north of Lake Pontchartrain. The Tunica Hills area is part of the East Gulf Coastal Plain. It has hills, bluffs, and deep ravines. The land is covered with **hardwood** forests and, in springtime, the pinks and whites of magnolias and dogwoods in bloom.

There are wetlands in the East Gulf Coastal Plain, too. They're filled with cypress and hardwood forests and a rich variety of birds and animals. There are also small, grassy prairies in this region.

The Mississippi Alluvial Plain

Where can you find a good swamp or marsh to explore? In the Mississippi Alluvial Plain. This region runs along the lower Mississippi River, from Arkansas all the way to the Gulf of Mexico. An **alluvial plain** is land created by dirt and **sediment** that was carried by a river and deposited in one place.

Over time, the Mississippi River has carried millions of tons of soil, rocks, and sediment and dumped them along its banks and where it flows into the Gulf. All that soil and sediment, combined with all that water, created areas that aren't quite land and aren't exactly all water, either. Louisiana is famous for these swamps and bayous. The largest wilderness swamp in the United States, the Atchafalaya Swamp, stretches through part of this area.

The Mississippi Alluvial Plain ends in a 13,000-square-mile (33,670-sq-km) area called the Mississippi Delta. That's huge—about one-quarter of the whole state is **delta**. From above, this looks like rich green land with thousands of tiny waterways snaking through it. Here the Mississippi River slows to a crawl. Thousands of small channels of water and mud inch through the delta. Land in the delta is the best farmland in the state. Two of Louisiana's biggest cities, New Orleans and Baton Rouge, are in the Delta.

More than **40 percent** of all the wetlands in the Lower **48 states** of the United States are in Louisiana.

WORDS TO KNOW

alluvial plain *an area that is created when sand, soil, and rocks are carried by water and dropped in a certain place*

sediment *material that is carried by water, wind, or glaciers*

delta *an alluvial deposit at the mouth of a river*

SEE IT HERE!

EXPLORE THE ATCHAFALAYA SWAMP

Being stuck in a swamp isn't what most people would consider fun. But Atchafalaya isn't your ordinary swamp. For one thing, it's the largest river swamp in North America. It's among the top 10 wilderness areas in the United States. The area is filled with cypress forests and teeming with animals. Visitors can take tour boats deep into the swamp. On a typical day, you might glimpse otters, mink, deer, squirrels, and up to 38 species of birds. Sometimes a keen-eyed visitor will spot an alligator lying motionless in the shallows.

Taking in the view at Longleaf Vista in Kisatchie National Forest—Louisiana's only national forest

West Gulf Coastal Plain

West of the Mississippi, the land changes from flat and wet to hilly and green. This area is the West Gulf Coastal Plain. It rises up from the Delta area, with impressive bluffs. Most of the hills and forests of Louisiana are in the northern areas. The highest point in the state, Driskill Mountain, is in the West Gulf Coastal Plain. So is the Kisatchie National Forest—the only national forest in Louisiana.

CLIMATE

Louisiana's semitropical climate, with warm temperatures and frequent rainfall, makes the state comfortable most of the year. Summers, though, can be brutal, especially near the coast. High humidity and high temperatures make the air wet and heavy during the summer.

The average temperatures in the state are very mild. In the northern areas, a typical July day is in the low 80s. Winter temperatures average around 53 degrees Fahrenheit (12 degrees Celsius). Every once in a while, snow will fall in the northern areas. But in the south, near the Gulf, it's likely to be sunny and warm most of the time, even in the winter.

Hurricane Season

In Louisiana, from mid-May to the end of November is hurricane season. During this period, everyone watches the weather for signs of these big storms. Sitting at the north coast of the Gulf of Mexico, Louisiana is a prime target for hurricanes. So if a hurricane that forms in the Atlantic Ocean veers into the Gulf, it can end up hitting Louisiana. Over the years, Louisiana has been battered by its share of these deadly storms.

One of the biggest natural disasters ever to strike the United States happened in late August 2005, when Hurricane Katrina slammed the coasts of Louisiana, Alabama, and Mississippi. Katrina was the sixth-strongest Atlantic hurricane ever recorded and the third-strongest hurricane to make landfall in the United States. The catastrophic Category-3 hurricane, with winds up to 127 miles per hour (204 kph), caused devastation along much of the north-central Gulf Coast of the United States, especially to the city of New Orleans.

Katrina ravaged much of the environment of the coastal areas. Storm **surges** eroded miles of beaches.

Weather Report

TEMPERATURE 114°F   TEMPERATURE -16°F

This chart shows record high and low temperatures in the state, average January and July temperatures, and average annual precipitation.

Record high temperature . . . . 114°F (46°C)
at Plain Dealing on August 10, 1936
Record low temperature . . . . −16°F (−27°C)
at Minden on February 13, 1899
Average temperature in January, New Orleans . . . . 53°F (12°C)
Average temperature in July, New Orleans . . . . 83°F (28°C)
Average annual precipitation, New Orleans . . . 62 inches (157 cm)
Average temperature in January, Shreveport . . . . . . 47°F (8°C)
Average temperature in July, Shreveport . . . . 83°F (28°C)
Average annual precipitation, Shreveport . . . . . 69 inches (175 cm)

Source: National Climatic Data Center, NESDIS, NOAA, U.S. Dept. of Commerce

WORD TO KNOW

surges *waves pushed onto land by the wind*

LOUISIANA

New Orleans

eye of the hurricane

This National Oceanic and Atmospheric Administration infrared satellite image shows the intensity of Hurricane Katrina.

Marshes and swamplands were ruined, and habitats for animals such as the brown pelican were damaged.

Because the storm was so deadly (1,836 people died, 1,577 in Louisiana), the World Meteorological Association has retired the name. No other hurricane will ever be called Katrina. Katrina is estimated to have caused $81.2 billion in damages, making it the costliest natural disaster in the history of the United States.

Just a month later, in September 2005, Louisiana was hit by another hurricane. Hurricane Rita made landfall at Johnson's Bayou, which is near the Texas border. It caused extensive damage to the region, and seven people were killed. In 2008, the state was hit by Hurricanes Ike and Gustav, and in 2012 it was affected by Hurricane Isaac. Along with a number of smaller storms, these hurricanes have caused billions of dollars of damage over the past several years.

The Levee System

The Mississippi River has been a source of life, and sometimes death, since people first settled near its banks. For centuries, people lived in harmony with the river—cultivating the fertile river lands and leaving the area in times of natural flooding. In modern times, with increasing populations and development along the river, the regular flooding became a problem. People tried to control the river by building embankments called **levees** along the river in attempts to stop the flooding.

Floods were always a threat to the city of New Orleans, which is located between two large bodies of water, the Gulf of Mexico and Lake Pontchartrain. In fact, some areas of New Orleans are actually several feet below the level of the water. Levees became a vital way to hold back the water in those areas. As more levees were constructed, areas of the city that had once been off-limits for building were turned into neighborhoods.

The early levees in New Orleans were mostly made of earth, sand, and fill dredged from canals and the sea. Newer levees are constructed of steel and concrete. Most of the time, the levees are effective. But Katrina was so powerful that many of the levees broke under the fury of the storm, and water flooded into the neighborhoods and streets of the city.

FAQ

Q8 WHICH ARE THE MOST DAMAGING HURRICANES EVER TO HIT LOUISIANA?

A8

Katrina	August 29, 2005	$108 billion
Ike	September 13, 2008	$29.5 billion
Rita	September 24, 2005	$10 billion
Gustav	September 1, 2008	$4.3 billion
Andrew	August 26, 1992	$1.6 billion
Juan	October 29, 1985	$1.5 billion

WORD TO KNOW

levees *wall-like embankments, often made of earth, built along a river to control flooding*

CAROLINE DORMON: FRIEND TO THE FORESTS

Growing up in the backwoods and forests near Natchitoches in the late 1800s, Caroline Dormon (1888–1971) loved to explore the woods and observe the plants and animals there. By the 1920s, Louisiana's forests were being cut down at a rapid rate. Through tireless work and sheer will, Dormon convinced the U.S. Forest Service to create Kisatchie National Forest in 1930. She later went on to write several books about Louisiana wildlife and plants, including *Wildflowers of Louisiana* and *Forests of Louisiana*. Today, her home at Briarwood is a museum and garden celebrating Dormon's passion for the outdoors.

? **Want to know more?** Visit www.factsfornow .scholastic.com and enter the keyword **Louisiana**.

The Atchafalaya Swamp is home to huge cypress trees.

PLANT LIFE

Almost half of Louisiana is covered with forests. The trees are a mix of hardwoods, such as oak, longleaf yellow pine, beech, and black walnut, and softwoods, such as spruce pine, in the north. Travel south, and you'll see huge live oaks draped with Spanish moss. Many wetlands in the Gulf area and the Mississippi Delta region boast huge cypress forests. Flowering trees such as magnolia and dogwood add bursts of color to the state.

Louisiana National Park Areas

This map shows some of Louisiana's parks, monuments, preserves, and other areas protected by the National Park Service.

ARKANSAS

Poverty Point NM

Shreveport

Monroe

Bayou Macon

Black

Mississippi

MISSISSIPPI

Red

Cane River Creole NHP

Toledo Bend Reservoir

El Camino Real de los Tejas NHT

Alexandria

TEXAS

Sabine

Calcasieu

Atchafalaya

★ Baton Rouge

Lake Pontchartrain

Lake Charles

Lafayette

Calcasieu Lake

New Orleans

New Orleans Jazz NHP

Sabine Lake

Intracoastal

Waterway

Jean Lafitte NHP & NPRES

Atchafalaya Bay

GULF OF MEXICO

N
W E
S

0   40 Miles
0   40 Kilometers

National Park area
NHP   National Historic Park
NHT   National Historic Trail
NM   National Monument
NPRES   National Preserve

ANIMAL LIFE

What's 13 feet (4 m) long, weighs up to 400 pounds (181 kilograms), and eats almost anything? If you guessed an alligator, you're right. Alligators love Louisiana's wetlands. These huge reptiles live throughout the state's swamps, bogs, lakes, ponds, rivers, and bayous.

Alligators may be one of the state's biggest wetlands residents, but they're not the only creatures living in the

American alligator

coastal areas that stretch throughout the Mississippi Delta. Animals such as mink, raccoons, otters, muskrats, bobcats, and beavers also make their homes in Louisiana's wetlands. Along the coastal marshes and on the islands live a huge variety of birds, including herons, egrets, brown pelicans, and snowy egrets. Freshwater areas such as lakes and rivers teem with fish, such as catfish. The most famous Louisiana water dwellers, besides alligators, are crawfish, freshwater crustaceans that look like small lobsters. Coastal beaches are home to sea life such as sea turtles, oysters, and sharks. Whales can sometimes be seen swimming along the coast.

One of the best-known coastal residents is the brown pelican. Pelicans nest along coastal islands and near the seashore. In the 1950s, pelicans almost became extinct, because of pollution and loss of habitat. Since then, conservationists have worked to restore the brown pelican to Louisiana. Today, they are no longer

Brown pelicans building nests on Camp Island

JOHN JAMES AUDUBON: WILDLIFE ARTIST

considered endangered. The eastern brown pelican is the state bird of Louisiana, and it can be seen on the state seal and quarter.

The forests are home to deer, squirrels, rabbits, bears, muskrats, mink, opossums, bobcats, and skunks. Birds that like the forests are quail, turkeys, woodcocks, and several species of ducks, including the mottled duck and wood duck. Bald eagles, once rare in Louisiana, now have a healthy population.

The Louisiana black bear once roamed the South, from southern Mississippi to parts of Texas. Now they're found only in a few areas of Louisiana. In the early 1990s, the black bear was declared an endangered species, mostly because of habitat loss and trapping. Today, several environmental groups and organizations such as the U.S. Fish and Wildlife Service are working together to increase the black bear population.

John James Audubon (1785–1851) wasn't born in Louisiana, and he lived in the state only a little while. But while there, he worked on one of the most beautiful and most popular nature books of all time. Audubon was born in Haiti and lived in Europe, then Philadelphia, and fell in love with birds and wildlife as a child. As an adult, he set out on a quest to record as many birds as he could. In 1821, he set up a studio and worked in New Orleans. His epic work, Birds of America, includes 435 life-size prints of birds, made from engraved plates that followed his original watercolor paintings. The book sealed his fame as an extraordinary American artist and naturalist.

? Want to know more? Visit www.factsfornow .scholastic.com and enter the keyword **Louisiana**.

PROTECTING THE LAND

Louisiana's wetlands are some of the most endangered areas in the United States. How could something so big be in trouble?

One reason is what scientists call a dead zone. The Mississippi River starts in Minnesota and flows for

LOUISIANA'S ENDANGERED SPECIES

While beautiful and lush with waterways and green forests, Louisiana is not without its share of endangered species. Among the endangered or threatened animals in Louisiana are the Louisiana black bear, manatee, black pine snake, gopher tortoise, Gulf sturgeon, and Mississippi gopher frog. Some of Louisiana's birds are also endangered, including the red-cockaded woodpecker and peregrine falcon. The whooping crane is nearly extinct in the state. Louisianans know that they need to protect the environment and help these and other animals to survive.

Black bear

2,300 miles (3,700 km) through cities, towns, wilderness, and farmlands. Not only does the river carry soil and sediment from the land, but it also carries toxic pollutants, such as chemicals and fertilizers, that have washed into the water. When the river empties into the Gulf of Mexico, these poisons are dumped along with it. Algae grows, using up all the oxygen in the water and killing everything else. Today, between 6,000 and 7,000 square miles (15,540 and 18,130 sq km) of water off the Louisiana coast are considered to be "dead."

The other reason Louisiana's wetlands and coastline are at risk is erosion, the wearing away of land by wind, water, and ice. Every year, between 25 and 35 square miles (65 and 90 sq km) of land are lost. Over time, people have built homes and towns in areas that were once regularly flooded by the Mississippi. The levees that have been built to prevent flooding in cities and towns along the Mississippi River have caused the river to straighten out. The river flows faster along its straight path, which keeps it from depositing the silt and debris that are needed to build up the wetlands. Now, instead of building up the wetlands, all the soil in the river is carried out to sea.

Mining and drilling for oil and **natural gas** have speeded up this erosion, too. To get these resources, companies have dug many canals through the wetlands. This isn't so bad—until a storm hits. Then these canals carry salty seawater much farther inland than it would normally go. The saltwater kills freshwater plants and animals, and the wetlands die.

One result of all this erosion is that parts of the Louisiana coastline are literally sinking. For millions of years, the wetlands had a natural cycle of slow erosion. Land would be washed away in storms and other

natural occurrences. Then it would be rebuilt and replenished from the soil carried by the Mississippi.

Today, eroded areas are not replenished, causing them to sink below the water. This phenomenon, known as **subsidence**, is starting to affect large parts of coastal Louisiana.

However, something can be done. Nature has its own way of healing the wetlands. Big hurricanes churn up the water in dead zones, mixing it with healthy water and bringing oxygen. People are helping, too. Communities upriver are trying to keep fertilizers and chemicals out of the Mississippi River. Citizens and lawmakers are discussing laws to control dredging and canal building. Some organizations are exploring new ways to help the wetlands, such as restoring specific marshlands and planting native grasses and plants. So far, programs such as these have saved about 5,000 acres (2,023 ha) of the wetlands. The people of Louisiana love their land, and they are working on ways to protect it.

Louisianans hope to preserve the environment for this mink and many other animals.

WORDS TO KNOW

natural gas *a gas that is formed in the earth when organic material decomposes under pressure*

subsidence *the state of eroded areas sinking underwater*

READ ABOUT

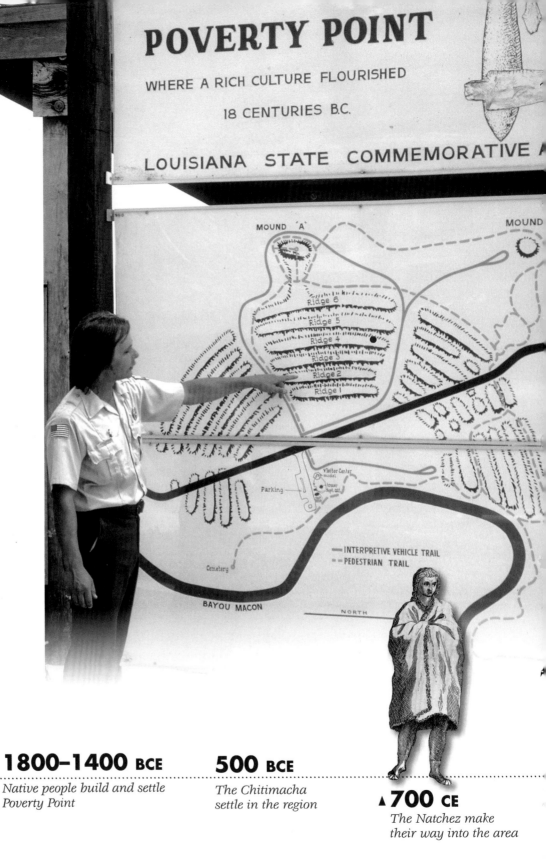

A Louisiana park ranger explains the layout of the Poverty Point National Monument.

POVERTY POINT

WHERE A RICH CULTURE FLOURISHED

18 CENTURIES B.C.

LOUISIANA STATE COMMEMORATIVE A

MOUND "A"   MOUND

Ridge 6
Ridge 5
Ridge 4
Ridge 3
Ridge 2
Ridge 1

Visitor Center
Parking
Cemetery

BAYOU MACON

NORTH

— INTERPRETIVE VEHICLE TRAIL
-- PEDESTRIAN TRAIL

1800–1400 BCE

Native people build and settle Poverty Point

500 BCE

The Chitimacha settle in the region

▲ **700 CE**

The Natchez make their way into the area

AREA

D B

LA. HWY. 577

CHAPTER TWO

FIRST PEOPLE

★

THERE'S A MYSTERY IN LOUISIANA. It covers more than 400 acres (162 ha). It's an ancient city, known as Poverty Point. It's a big mystery because very little is known about the people who built it. Poverty Point is one of the largest and most important ancient Native American sites ever found in North America. However, nothing much is left of this city today except some earthen mounds and a few stone artifacts.

900
The Caddo people arrive

1100–1400 ▶
The Caddo produce pottery

1500s
Europeans begin to arrive, leading to the demise of the region's Native peoples.

NAMING POVERTY POINT

How did Poverty Point get its name? As you might guess, the name does not come from the people who built it—no one knows what it was called back then. The area got its name in 1843 from Phillip Guier, a cotton planter who'd bought the land and built a plantation nearby. His crops did so poorly that he called his farm Poverty Point.

WORD TO KNOW

radiocarbon dating *a process that dates an object by counting its radioactive decay of carbon*

SEE IT HERE!

POVERTY POINT NATIONAL MONUMENT

It takes a minute to realize what you're looking at when you first visit Poverty Point National Monument. The city covers more than 400 acres (162 ha). That's the size of 303 football fields. Six earthen mounds 100 feet (30 m) wide are laid out in rings around an enormous courtyard.

Climb the observation tower to see the best part of Poverty Point: Three earthen mounds built in the shape of a bird in flight. The people who built this giant bird didn't have bulldozers or even shovels. They dug all that dirt with sticks and carried it in baskets.

UNDERSTANDING POVERTY POINT

From artifacts that were found all around Poverty Point, scientists learned that a Native American settlement had once existed in the northeastern corner of Louisiana. Then, in the 1950s, scientists from the American Museum of Natural History discovered a 20-year-old photograph of the area that had been taken from the air. They were stunned to see the outline of an enormous city laid out in a half circle. Until then, they had no idea how huge or how old Poverty Point actually was.

Scientists used a technique called **radiocarbon dating** to figure out the age of Poverty Point's artifacts. They estimated that Poverty Point must have been built sometime between 1800 and 1400 BCE. That makes it older than any other site its size in the Western Hemisphere.

Since the 1950s, archaeologists have discovered a lot about the people who lived at Poverty Point from the things they left behind. They hunted with darts and spears instead of bows and arrows. They made pottery and created tools out of stone. They carved images of animals out of stone as well. They traded with other Native Americans in northern areas of the United States. And they had their own religious beliefs.

But much more remains a mystery. Where did these people come from? How did they construct such a huge, advanced city at a time when other Native people were still living in small groups? And, strangest of all, what happened to them? If you become an archaeologist, maybe you can help solve the puzzles of Poverty Point.

WOW

It took about 1.5 million tons of earth and rocks to build the mounds at Poverty Point!

NATIVE PEOPLES OF LOUISIANA

About 900 to 1,300 years after the settlement at Poverty Point, a group called the Chitimacha had settled in Louisiana. Another 1,200 years passed before they were joined by the Natchez, in around 700 CE. A third group, the Caddo, arrived 200 years later. Each of the three groups had its own special traditions and religious practices, territories, and languages. And within each group were thousands of people who were as individual as people are today.

These groups varied. Some were small clans of hunters, and others were huge farming villages.

This is an example of Caddo pottery. The Caddo arrived in the region around 900 CE.

Native American Peoples
(Before European Contact)

This map shows the general area of Native American peoples before European settlers arrived.

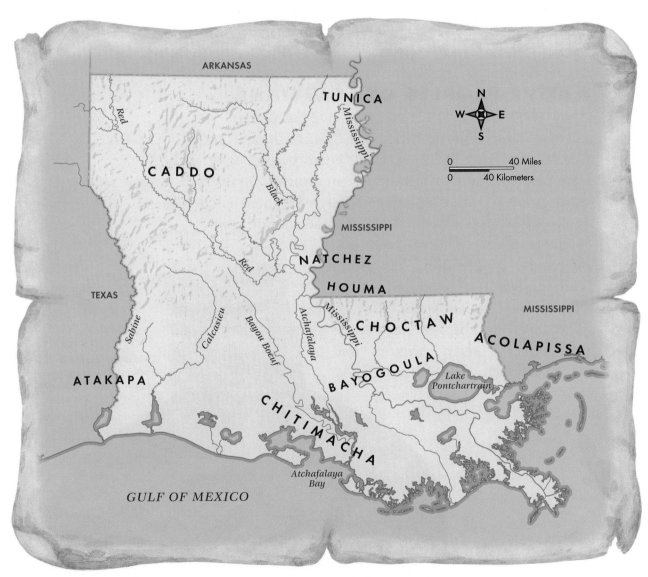

The people were in contact with one another all the time, trading goods, sharing information, and sometimes working together to harvest crops or to hunt.

Within the groups, men generally hunted, defended the village, built homes and canoes, and crafted tools and other objects. Women cared for children, prepared food, took care of the crops, and made their families colorful clothing from feathers, bark, hides, and furs. People ate meat and fish, vegetables, fruits, and nuts. They wore necklaces, bracelets, armbands, and rings made from shells, bones, pearls, and copper.

TRADITIONAL LIFESTYLES

The Atakapa lived mainly along the coasts and wetlands of southwestern Louisiana and southeastern Texas. They were very good alligator hunters. They used alligators for meat, oil, and hides. (Alligator oil was a great insect repellent!) The Atakapa were short and sturdy. Like many Native people, they wore clothing made of animal skins and buffalo hides. Parents molded baby carriers out of wet bark, then let it dry. They made diapers out of Spanish moss. They probably lived in houses with palmetto-leaf roofs.

Another group was the Tunica. When Europeans first described them in 1699, Tunica land covered parts of modern-day Arkansas, Louisiana, and Mississippi. The Tunica were continually moving around and settling in new areas. Once they found a place they liked, they built villages and grew crops. The people lived in conical-shaped houses made from cane stalks and wood.

No one knows much about the earliest Muskegon Indians in Louisiana, because they didn't survive long after Europeans arrived. (Many caught deadly diseases from the Europeans.) A few Muskegon people lived in

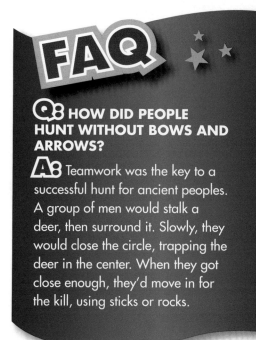

FAQ

Q8 HOW DID PEOPLE HUNT WITHOUT BOWS AND ARROWS?

A8 Teamwork was the key to a successful hunt for ancient peoples. A group of men would stalk a deer, then surround it. Slowly, they would close the circle, trapping the deer in the center. When they got close enough, they'd move in for the kill, using sticks or rocks.

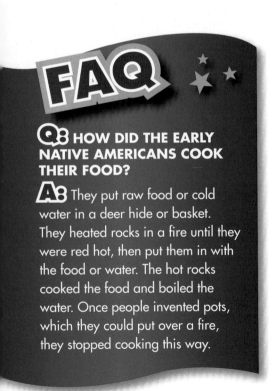

A group of Choctaw and Caddo playing a game now known as lacrosse

FAQ ★ ★ ★

Q8 HOW DID THE EARLY NATIVE AMERICANS COOK THEIR FOOD?

A8 They put raw food or cold water in a deer hide or basket. They heated rocks in a fire until they were red hot, then put them in with the food or water. The hot rocks cooked the food and boiled the water. Once people invented pots, which they could put over a fire, they stopped cooking this way.

the Delta region near Louisiana, and they were closely related to the Choctaw group of present-day Mississippi and Alabama. The Houma were a Muskegon group who lived in a large village along the Mississippi River. Another Muskegon group, the Bayogoula, lived near modern-day Lake Pontchartrain. The alligator was their sacred symbol.

The Acolapissa was a group that lived in the coastal lagoons and along the Pearl and Mississippi rivers. Their name in the Choctaw language means "those who listen and see." These Indians would be among the first people to come into regular contact with French explorers.

The Natchez settlements stretched along both sides of the Mississippi River, including a big chunk of Louisiana. Their biggest city included a sacred temple, huge earthen mounds, and a central square where the people held ceremonies and played games. The Natchez people raised fields of corn, beans, squash, tobacco, and other crops. The men of the group hunted and fished. The leader of the Natchez, called the Great

Sun, lived in a big house on top of one of the mounds and was worshipped as a god. His feet were never allowed to touch the ground! When he wanted to go somewhere, servants carried him on a litter, a type of bed or chair carried on two poles.

Deep in the swamps and delta lands west of the Mississippi River, 15 villages with about 500 people each made up the large and powerful Chitimacha nation. At the beginning of the 1700s, more than 3,000 Chitimachas lived in large villages throughout most of the area below modern-day New Orleans. Each village had its own leaders, but a grand chief ruled over everyone. He lived at the main Chitimacha village near present-day Charenton, Louisiana. The men and women were expert woodcarvers and made toys for their children. They were also skilled metalworkers, using copper to make tools.

The Caddo people lived along the modern-day Texas-Louisiana border and into parts of Arkansas. This powerful nation was loosely divided into three **confederacies**: the Hasini in Texas, the Kadohadacho, whose lands included northwest Louisiana and southern Arkansas, and the Natchitoches, who lived in the Red River valley near present-day Nachitoches. Some of the individual groups that lived in Louisiana included the Adai, Doustioni, Ouachita, and Yatasi.

Each group had its own government, which included offi-

A chunkey stone

Picture Yourself...

Playing Chunkey

You're standing beside a field twice the size of a football field. Fans have traveled for days and camped out just to see you, because *you* are a chunkey champion. Next to your opponent—a member of a different Indian group—you stand on one end of a field. Each of you is holding a spear. The referee rolls a stone out onto the field. You and your opponents throw your spears, hoping to hit the spot where the stone will eventually stop. You'll win if you come closest, without hitting the stone.

You've done it again! Fans are screaming. Your parents are in the stands, waving and cheering. You've won not only prizes, but also the pride of being champion.

Chunkey dates back to 1300 to 1600 CE. Chunkey fields have been found in Native American villages all over the South, showing how popular the game was. One player was even buried with a chunkey stone. He was probably a grand champion!

MINI-BIO

MELISSA DARDEN: KEEPING AN ANCIENT ART ALIVE

The Chitimacha people are highly skilled basket makers. Today, only four people know how to weave these distinctive baskets. Melissa Darden (c. 1969–) is one of them. Darden began making baskets in 1992. Her grandmother, Lydia, first taught her the complex techniques of weaving, and Melissa would go to museums and take pictures of as many baskets as she could find to study the beautiful designs. She makes them the traditional way: using only a knife, her hands, and her teeth. Many Louisiana festivals have featured her work.

 Want to know more? Visit www.factsfornow .scholastic.com. Enter the keyword **Louisiana** and look for the Biography logo.

Chitimacha basket

cials, chiefs, and spiritual leaders. The leader of all the groups in a confederacy was the Grand Caddi. The Caddo were savvy traders who saw the influx of Europeans as an opportunity: new customers for their goods such as hides, salt, and horses.

The Caddo also produced fine pottery. Between 1100 and 1400 CE, they produced some of their most beautiful pieces.

DEVASTATION OF NATIVE GROUPS

In the 1500s, Europeans from France and Spain began arriving in North America, first as explorers, then as conquerors. As powerful as many of the native Louisianans were, they were no match for European guns—or European diseases. Sickness and war eventually led to the demise of many of Louisiana's Native peoples. By the 1700s, most Native American groups were gone and only six different groups remained in Louisiana: the Tunica, the Atakapa, the Natchez, the Muskegon, the Chitimacha, and the Caddo.

Around 1700, an epidemic wiped out most of the Acolapissa. The survivors scattered, joining other villages. After Europeans arrived, many Tunica had relocated to Texas and Mississippi and joined with groups there. Remaining Tunica joined with other groups such as the Atakapa. By 1805, the Atakapa—once several thousand strong—were reduced to only 175; 100 years later, only nine were left.

A Choctaw encampment along the Mississippi River

The Natchez suffered from wars with and diseases brought by the French. Those who survived the warfare and disease fled and joined others such as the Chickasaw, Creek, Catawba, and Cherokee. In the late 1600s, the French decided they wanted Chitimacha lands and started a war that lasted 12 years. The Chitimacha were almost wiped out. As more Europeans settled onto Caddoan lands, the Native Americans were overwhelmed. In 1834, the Caddo sold 1 million acres (405,000 ha) of their land to the United States and eventually moved to present-day Oklahoma.

Only a handful of survivors from each village managed to escape death or disease. Many sought refuge with other area peoples, while others moved far away. Years later, those survivors regrouped and slowly rebuilt a few of the Louisiana villages that had once been destroyed. Today, village members work to bring back the memories, culture, and traditions of their people.

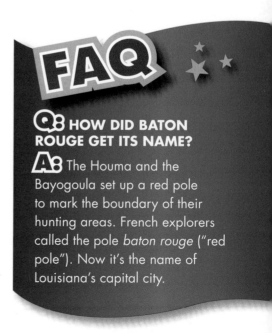

FAQ

Q8 HOW DID BATON ROUGE GET ITS NAME?

A8 The Houma and the Bayogoula set up a red pole to mark the boundary of their hunting areas. French explorers called the pole *baton rouge* ("red pole"). Now it's the name of Louisiana's capital city.

READ ABOUT

11

6

13

12

10

5

13

2

16

GOLFE DE MEXIQUE

Basset

Ste Geneviè

re du Mississipi	5. Nouveau Fort Louis	LE MISSISSIPI	9. Pensacola
le Orleans	6. Vieux Fort Louis	ou la Louisiane	10. Mobile Riv
nt chartrain	7. Isle Dauphine	dans l'Amerique	11. Governado
Maurepas	8. Isle de la chandeleur	Septentrionale.	12. Baye de S

A map of
Louisiana along
the Gulf of Mexico,
mid-1700s

1 PTA   IV CENTENARIO DE FLORIDA
CABEZA
DE VACA
CORREOS
ESPAÑA

1519

*Alonso Álvarez de Pineda
maps the Gulf Coast*

1528 ▲

*Alvar Nuñez Cabeza de
Vaca wanders through
Louisiana*

1682

*Natchez Indians make first
contact with white explorer
René-Robert Cavelier, Sieur
de La Salle*

CHAPTER THREE

EXPLORATION AND SETTLEMENT

★

A LONSO ÁLVAREZ DE PINEDA LED AN IMPORTANT SPANISH EXPEDITION. In 1519, Pineda was hired by the Spanish governor of Jamaica, Francisco de Garay, to map the coast of the Gulf of Mexico. Pineda discovered the mouth of a great river that he named Rio de las Palmas, which means "river of palms." This river was probably the Mississippi. And Pineda was the first European to see and map the coast of Louisiana.

1699

Pierre Le Moyne, Sieur d'Iberville, founds Fort Maurepas

1718 ▶

Jean-Baptiste Le Moyne, Sieur de Bienville, founds New Orleans

1763

Spain wins control of Louisiana

Spanish explorer Alvar Nuñez Cabeza de Vaca and his men rest during their expedition of the Gulf Coast region.

EUROPEAN EXPLORERS

The Spanish rulers weren't interested in swamps and bayous. They ignored Pineda's recommendations to build settlements. For many years, explorers who reached Louisiana came by accident or just passed through on their way somewhere else. In 1528, Alvar Nuñez Cabeza de Vaca was trying to sail from Florida to Mexico when he and his men were shipwrecked on the Gulf Coast. Most of his crew died, but Cabeza de Vaca spent six years wandering and trying to figure out how to return to Mexico. He and three companions eventually made it there. Cabeza de Vaca wrote

European Exploration of Louisiana

The colored arrows on this map show the routes taken by explorers between 1541 and 1699.

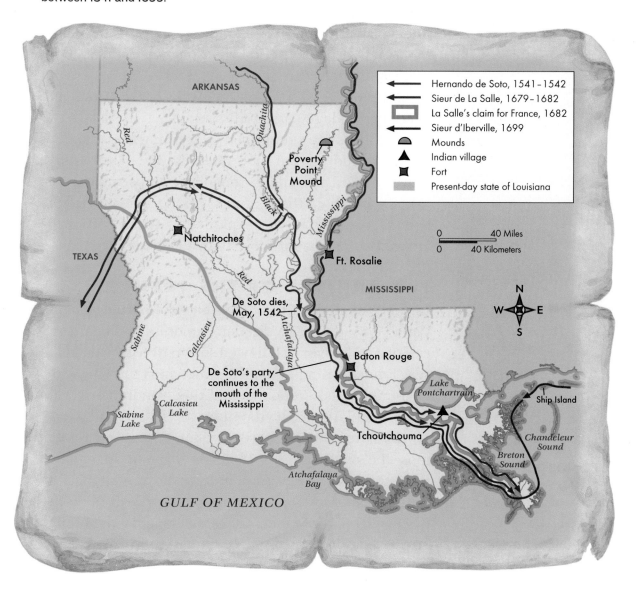

ARKANSAS

Red

Ouachita

Poverty Point Mound

Black

Mississippi

TEXAS

Natchitoches

Red

Ft. Rosalie

MISSISSIPPI

De Soto dies, May, 1542

Atchafalaya

Baton Rouge

De Soto's party continues to the mouth of the Mississippi

Lake Pontchartrain

Ship Island

Sabine

Calcasieu

Tchoutchouma

Chandeleur Sound

Breton Sound

Calcasieu Lake

Sabine Lake

Atchafalaya Bay

GULF OF MEXICO

Legend:
- Hernando de Soto, 1541–1542
- Sieur de La Salle, 1679–1682
- La Salle's claim for France, 1682
- Sieur d'Iberville, 1699
- Mounds
- Indian village
- Fort
- Present-day state of Louisiana

0   40 Miles
0   40 Kilometers

N W E S

THE EXPLORER WHO DISAPPEARED

In 1519, Alonso Álvarez de Pineda commanded a Spanish expedition that mapped the Gulf of Mexico. He described a very large river, which could have been the Mississippi. His voyages also proved that Florida was not an island, which was news to Europe at the time. Pineda and his crew sailed up the river and entered several Native American villages. The people probably welcomed him, because the expedition stayed for weeks, cleaning and repairing their ships. Pineda and many of his crew members decided to stay and build a settlement.

What happened to Pineda is a mystery. A few months later, another Spanish ship came back to find the settlement controlled by Native Americans. There was no sign of Pineda.

WORDS TO KNOW

colonized *created colonies, which are settlements that are controlled by another government*

exposure *a condition of not being protected from severe weather*

a long report on everything he had seen and done. There's no proof that he saw Louisiana, but he did record information about what became the southern United States.

Hernando de Soto and his army next marched through what are now the Carolinas, Tennessee, Alabama, Mississippi, Arkansas, and Louisiana on a trip that lasted more than three years. In 1541, he reached the Mississippi River. He died of a fever on the banks of the Mississippi near present-day Natchez, Mississippi.

De Soto's men described everything they encountered, including the hot climate, the "unfriendly" Native Americans, and the deadly swamps and bayous. Understandably, their reports didn't encourage the Spanish crown to further explore the region. Europeans ignored Louisiana for more than 100 years.

THE ARRIVAL OF THE FRENCH

In the meantime, the French had **colonized** areas of Canada. By the 1670s, French explorers had heard stories of a wide river that flowed south from Canada to the sea. France's King Louis XIV, known as the Sun King, encouraged the French to find this wondrous river, in order to enlarge his own empire.

Explorer René-Robert Cavelier, Sieur de La Salle, took the challenge. In 1682, his expedition reached the mouth of the Mississippi, an area inhabited by the Natchez Indians, and claimed it, and all the lands drained by it, for France. La Salle persuaded the French crown to support a colony in Louisiana. A small settlement called Fort Saint Louis was built. However, the settlement was not a success. Colonists died of starvation, of **exposure**, or in battles with Native Americans. By 1689, Fort Saint Louis lay in ruins.

French explorer René-Robert Cavelier, Sieur de La Salle, and his expedition enter the Louisiana region, by way of the Mississippi River.

The next French settlement in Louisiana was built by explorer Pierre Le Moyne, Sieur d'Iberville. In 1699, he sailed into the Gulf of Mexico and established a settlement on the coast rather than on the river, as La Salle had done. Le Moyne worried that large ships would get stuck entering the mouth of the river.

The French built several settlements, but all of them failed. The land wasn't good for crops. Insects and wild animals made life miserable. Still the French kept at it. In 1718, Jean-Baptiste Le Moyne, Sieur de Bienville, founded a settlement he named New Orleans, in honor of the Duke of Orleans.

40

PIERRE LE MOYNE, SIEUR D'IBERVILLE: LEGENDARY SOLDIER

Pierre Le Moyne, Sieur d'Iberville (1661–1706) was born in Canada. By 1686, he had become a seasoned soldier and sailor. In 1697, the French government chose him to colonize Louisiana. He arrived at the mouth of the Mississippi on March 2, 1699, and founded Fort Maurepas. He lived in the new colony until 1702, then went off to fight for France against the English. Four years later, he died in what is now Havana, Cuba, of yellow fever.

? Want to know more? Visit www.factsfornow.scholastic.com and enter the keyword **Louisiana**.

FOUNDING OF NEW ORLEANS

Swampy. Buggy. Hot. The southeastern tip of Louisiana was all of these things. So it was remarkable that Le Moyne would seek to build a city there. In 1718, after other French settlements failed, he thought he'd try a place on some high ground between the Mississippi and Lake Pontchartrain. It was already a village where many Native Americans traded goods because it was easy to carry boats between the two waterways.

This map shows a plan for New Orleans as it appeared in 1718 to 1720.

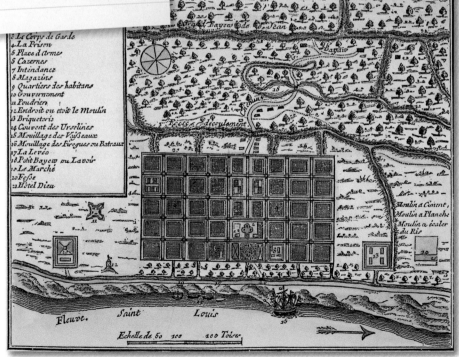

Once he had decided on the location, Le Moyne brought in a team of about 50 men to clear the forests and underbrush. A French engineer named Adrien de Pauger arrived to design and oversee the construction. He created the street plan that can still be seen in the French Quarter today. Pauger also included a levee system to protect the city from flooding.

New Orleans soon became the center of a new regional trade network. Shops and markets sprang up for selling all the goods that came through.

MORE PEOPLE IN A NEW LAND

After the death of King Louis XIV of France, no one in the French government wanted to take on the Louisiana Colony. In 1719, the French government turned it over to a Scotsman named John Law.

Under Law's leadership, Louisiana became prosperous. He advertised in Europe for colonists. Starting in 1721, more than 2,000 German immigrants settled in the colony. Law also shipped convicts from French prisons to the colony. While some of them were hardened criminals, most were people looking for a new start. Law's rule lasted only a few years, though. Crop failures, Indian wars, and money issues forced him to return the colony to the French government.

FRENCH AND INDIAN WAR

In the 1750s, France and Great Britain were part of a European conflict known as the French and Indian War (or the Seven Years' War). By 1756, Spain had joined the conflict. It lasted until 1763, when France and Spain were defeated. As part of the peace agreement, France gave Spain Louisiana, which the Spanish controlled for the next 38 years.

MINI-BIO

BERNARDO GÁLVEZ: WAR HERO

The American colonists who defeated Great Britain in the Revolutionary War could not have won without the help of the Spanish governor of Louisiana, Bernardo Gálvez (1746–1786). Gálvez was born in Málaga, Spain, and joined the Spanish army as a teenager. On January 1, 1777, he became governor of Louisiana.

In 1779, Spain came to the aid of the American colonists. That year, Gálvez defeated the British in Louisiana. The next year, he captured the British stronghold of Fort Charlotte in Mobile, Alabama. His greatest moment in the Revolutionary War came when he commanded 7,000 men in an attack against the British in Pensacola, Florida. He successfully captured Pensacola. Gálvez is considered the greatest Spanish hero of the American Revolution.

? **Want to know more?** Visit www.factsfornow .scholastic.com and enter the keyword **Louisiana**.

Under Spain, Louisiana's population grew with immigrants from France, Great Britain, Spain, and the Canary Islands. Acadians came from Canada, and free Africans came from Haiti and other Caribbean colonies. Enslaved people made up half of the population. By the start of the 19th century, there were about 50,000 people in Louisiana, with more than 10,000 in New Orleans.

THE LOUISIANA ACADIANS

The Acadians were French colonists who settled in Canada in the early 1600s. Their settlement, in an area known as Acadia, thrived for about 150 years. In the mid-1700s, the British government took over Canada and forcibly removed all the French colonists. The British burned Acadian farms and separated Acadian families, deporting them to faraway places. The first Acadians arrived in Louisiana by way of New York in 1754. In the 1760s, hundreds more came. These displaced French colonists brought their culture and language with them. Expert farmers and fishers, they continued their work in Louisiana. They settled in "the Cajun prairie," an area that no one else wanted.

Over time, the Acadians in Louisiana became known as Cajuns. They intermarried with the Spanish,

English, and Africans, and these cultures influenced the Cajun way of life, especially the language. Today, the Cajun language is a rich mix of French, English, and other tongues.

REASONS FOR GROWTH

How did Louisiana grow so fast? Spain encouraged immigration to Louisiana. Agriculture began to thrive once people discovered how rich and fertile the land in the Mississippi Delta was. Farmers grew so prosperous that they turned small farms into large plantations. Prosperity brought a spirit of excitement to Louisiana and to New Orleans, which drew people in.

Louisiana was also a place where some people felt free to do what they wanted with their lives. Free blacks were allowed to open businesses or start farms, unlike blacks in other parts of the United States at the time. Europeans from many countries found that they were more alike than different. People of all backgrounds owned businesses in New Orleans and worked together to prosper.

THE CREOLES

The term *Creole* has always been confusing—because it can mean different things to different people. When Europeans first arrived in the Americas, Portuguese colonists used the word to describe a slave of African descent. The Spanish used the word *criollo* to refer to anyone of either African or European descent who was born in the Americas. By the 19th century, *Creole* described mixed-race people. Eventually, the name became used for freeborn people of color in Louisiana. After the Civil War, Creoles often intermarried with Cajuns and blended into Cajun culture. Today, *Creole* often refers to Louisianans of full or mixed African heritage.

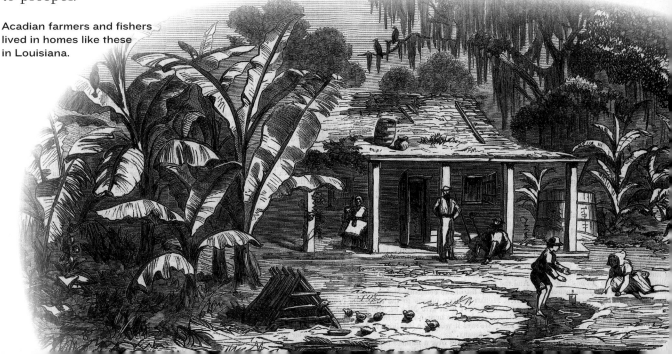

Acadian farmers and fishers lived in homes like these in Louisiana.

READ ABOUT

In 1803, the Louisiana Purchase doubled the size of the United States overnight. This is the agreement.

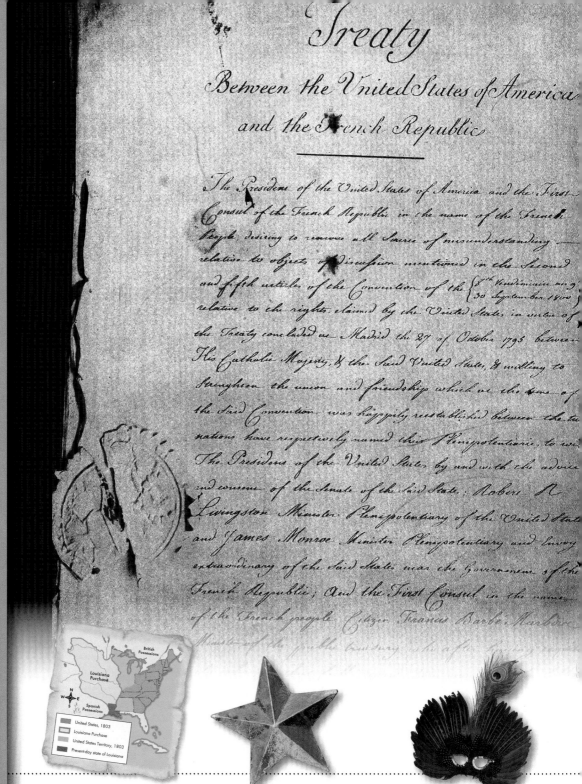

Treaty

Between the United States of America and the French Republic

▲ **1803**
The United States obtains the land known as the Louisiana Purchase for $15 million

▲ **1812**
Louisiana becomes the 18th state

1838 ▲
The first Mardi Gras in New Orleans is held

CHAPTER FOUR

GROWTH AND CHANGE

★

IN THE EARLY 1800S, NAPOLEON BONAPARTE OF FRANCE WAS ONE OF THE MOST SUCCESSFUL MILITARY COMMANDERS IN THE WORLD. His ambition for power and desperation for money would change the fate of Louisiana forever. In 1800, Napoleon was busy conquering Europe. But his dream was to take Louisiana back from Spain and create a new French empire in the Americas.

1861

Louisiana secedes from the Union, and the Civil War begins

1879 ▸

Baton Rouge becomes Louisiana's state capital

1909

Louisiana's first sulfur mine opens

Q8 HOW BIG WAS THE LOUISIANA PURCHASE?

A8 The Louisiana Purchase covered 828,000 square miles (2,144,520 sq km) of land, stretching east to west from the Mississippi River to the Rocky Mountains and north to south from Canada to the Gulf of Mexico. The new land doubled the size of the United States—and cost only four cents an acre! In time, the Louisiana Purchase would be carved into the states of Montana, Wyoming, North Dakota, South Dakota, Minnesota, Iowa, Missouri, Nebraska, Kansas, New Mexico, Oklahoma, Texas, Arkansas, and Louisiana. Now that's a lot of land!

THE LOUISIANA PURCHASE

In the 1800s, Napoleon convinced Spain to give Louisiana back to France in a secret agreement called the Treaty of Ildefonso. But a successful slave rebellion in the French colony of Haiti, and the enormous cost of trying to conquer Europe, preoccupied Napoleon. When the United States offered to purchase New Orleans from France, Napoleon countered with an offer to sell the entire Louisiana territory. The price was set at $15 million, and the Louisiana Purchase was signed on May 2, 1803.

After the Louisiana Purchase, Louisiana continued to prosper. Ships brought goods, supplies, and people to New Orleans. Slaves were also brought in by these ships. Soon New Orleans became the second-largest port city in the United States, after New York City. On April 30, 1812, Louisiana became the 18th state after the U.S. Congress approved its constitution. The territorial governor, William Charles Cole Claiborne, was elected the first governor of the state of Louisiana.

IMMIGRANTS FROM MANY LANDS

French immigrants had made Louisiana home since the earliest days of the colony, and they kept arriving throughout the 19th century. More French immigrants settled in New Orleans than in any other city in the United States. Ties between Louisiana and France remained strong, and it was not unusual for Louisianans, both black and white, to travel to France regularly.

By 1810, more than 10,000 refugees from the slave revolt in Haiti (then Saint-Domingue) had fled to New Orleans, doubling the population of the city. This group of immigrants included whites, free blacks, and slaves. Between 1806 and 1809, 4,000 Africans and 2,000 Europeans arrived from the Spanish West Indies.

Louisiana Purchase

This map shows the area (in yellow) that made up the Louisiana Purchase and the present-day state of Louisiana (in orange).

Louisiana was a destination for 19th-century Europeans fleeing poverty, religious persecution, or just boredom. It was less expensive for immigrants to sail to New Orleans than to other ports, such as New York City. For immigrants heading farther west, New Orleans was the ideal starting point. Steamboats traveled up the Mississippi to Saint Louis and other cities, where there were wagon trains headed west. A Louisiana riverboat to the Midwest cost less and took less time than overland transportation from Eastern cities.

Louisiana: From Territory to Statehood
(1804–1812)

This map shows the original Louisiana territory and the area (in yellow) that became the state of Louisiana in 1812.

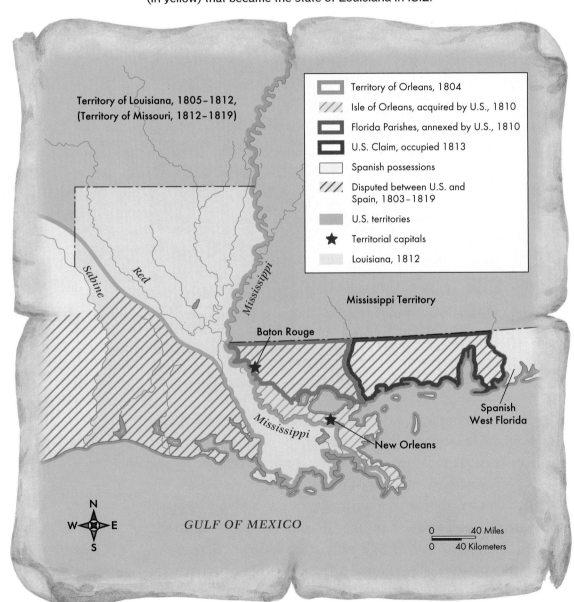

Territory of Louisiana, 1805–1812, (Territory of Missouri, 1812–1819)

▭	Territory of Orleans, 1804
▨	Isle of Orleans, acquired by U.S., 1810
▭	Florida Parishes, annexed by U.S., 1810
▭	U.S. Claim, occupied 1813
▭	Spanish possessions
▨	Disputed between U.S. and Spain, 1803–1819
▭	U.S. territories
★	Territorial capitals
▭	Louisiana, 1812

Sabine

Red

Mississippi

Mississippi Territory

Baton Rouge

Mississippi

Spanish West Florida

New Orleans

N   W   E   S

GULF OF MEXICO

0 ___ 40 Miles
0 ___ 40 Kilometers

Between 1820 and 1860, about 180,000 Germans arrived in New Orleans. Most of these new immigrants traveled on to the Midwest, then to California. But many Germans stayed in Louisiana. In 1860, German immigrants made up about one-tenth of New Orleans's population.

German immigrants opened restaurants, dance halls, and theaters. German musicians introduced a new instrument, the accordion, to the sound of New Orleans. Later, Cajun musicians adopted the accordion, adding its bright sound to their musical mix.

Irish immigrants were among the earliest European settlers to make a home in Louisiana. A big wave of Irish immigrants arrived in New Orleans in the 1830s and 1840s, during and after the Irish Potato **Famine**. By 1860, there were more than 24,000 Irish immigrants in New Orleans. Many of them were professionals such as teachers, lawyers, doctors, architects, and printers. Others took less-skilled work as domestic help or on the railroads and docks.

THE WAR OF 1812 AND THE BATTLE OF NEW ORLEANS

Just a few months before Louisiana became a state, the United States declared war on Great Britain, in part to remove Britain's remaining control in North America. The War of 1812 lasted nearly three years. The United States was convinced that the British would attack New Orleans, so General Andrew Jackson and his troops arrived to defend the city.

On January 8, 1815, Jackson and his men—along with two African American military units, Native Americans, and Jean Lafitte and other pirates— soundly defeated the British forces trying to capture

PIRATES OF THE GULF

Smugglers and pirates had been fixtures in Louisiana throughout the 18th century. Pirates of all nationalities smuggled goods through the numerous swamps, bayous, and rivers. They also smuggled slaves.

One of the more infamous pirates was Jean Lafitte. But he may have been better known for the assistance he gave to American forces during the War of 1812. At the Battle of New Orleans on January 8, 1815, Lafitte and his men helped General Andrew Jackson's army soundly defeat the British forces. After the war, Lafitte worked for the Spanish government and founded a colony in Galveston, Texas. From there, he continued his smuggling operations, but he always remained loyal to the United States.

WORD TO KNOW

famine *drastic loss of food, causing starvation and death*

Thousands of Jewish people from Germany, Spain, and France immigrated to Louisiana in the 19th century. In fact, by 1860, Louisiana was home to the largest Jewish population in the South.

New Orleans. However, neither Jackson nor the British forces knew that the United States and Britain had already signed a peace treaty. Still, his victory in the Battle of New Orleans is considered one of the greatest American military victories because of the bravery and courage Jackson's small army showed in defeating the larger British force.

THE RISE OF SLAVERY IN LOUISIANA

The invention of the cotton gin in 1794 and advances in sugarcane processing made growing and harvesting those crops easier and more profitable.

To make money, plantation owners would need a cheap labor force to plant, tend, and harvest their fields. Like other southern states, Louisiana's economy became dependent on unpaid labor of enslaved Africans. The system made a small number of plantation owners wealthy, and their profits gave them enormous political power.

Sugarcane, Louisiana's cash crop, was usually harvested by enslaved people from Africa.

Louisiana planters and slave owners even used enslaved children in the fields.

To persuade poor whites to support their system, plantation owners promoted the idea that whites were superior to blacks. The poverty, low wages, and lack of education of poor whites put them just above the misery of slaves. But once persuaded that they were members of "a master race," poor whites did the planters' bidding. They even did their dirty work, serving in nightly slave patrols for six cents an hour.

By 1850, slaves made up almost half of Louisiana's total population. Enslaved workers toiled on farms that ranged in size from sugar plantations of hundreds of acres to small tobacco farms of only a few acres. Cotton picking was difficult, finger-splitting work. Each picker was expected to harvest up to 150 pounds (68 kg) of cotton each day, no matter how long it took.

WOW

In 1811, 500 enslaved men and women rebelled and marched from Saint John the Baptist Parish to New Orleans. They staged one of the largest slave revolts in North American history. It took local militia units and federal troops to crush their bid for liberty.

T HART SLAVES

Slaves wait to be sold at a New Orleans auction in 1861.

The United States had outlawed importing kid-napped Africans in 1808, so most of the slaves who were brought to New Orleans came from other states. The port city of New Orleans had become the South's largest slave-trading center by 1850. Slaves were sold at public auction, and the city had 25 slave auction houses.

Slave owners and their huge plantations made up only a small part of the economy of Louisiana, but they controlled the wealth and power. Louisiana's planters were among the wealthiest in the South. Although most of the plantation owners were white, there were many free black farm owners. Some became wealthy planters, as well, and even owned slaves. Free people of color were numerous in New Orleans.

THE CIVIL WAR'S IMPACT

After the Northern states outlawed slavery, tensions between North and South ran high. Southern states believed they had the right to govern themselves, make their own laws, and treat slaves as property. At that time, states considered themselves more powerful than the federal government. When Southern planters called for states' rights, they really wanted the right to spread their system into the western United States.

These tensions came to a head in 1860, when Abraham Lincoln was elected president. Lincoln's election meant planters would not be permitted to bring slaves into western territories. Because Lincoln opposed their point of view, Southern states organized to topple his government. On January 26, 1861, Louisiana **seceded** from the Union to join what became known as the Confederacy.

Louisiana sent more than 23,000 troops to the Confederate army. In 1862, early in the war, Union forces invaded New Orleans and kept it under their control until the war ended in 1865. Few battles were fought in Louisiana.

Before the Civil War (1861–1865), Louisiana's population had swelled to more than 700,000. After the Civil War ended, foreign immigration to Louisiana dropped off considerably. The war had disrupted shipping and passenger service to New Orleans, and it never recovered. The Transcontinental Railroad, which was completed in 1869, connected the nation's East and West coasts by train, making travel across the country cheap and fast. After the war, moving to Louisiana became less desirable because there were few good manufacturing jobs and other professions. Immigrants began bypassing New Orleans and Louisiana for other places with better opportunities.

WORDS TO KNOW

seceded *withdrew from a group*

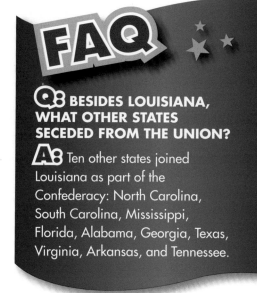

Q8 BESIDES LOUISIANA, WHAT OTHER STATES SECEDED FROM THE UNION?

A8 Ten other states joined Louisiana as part of the Confederacy: North Carolina, South Carolina, Mississippi, Florida, Alabama, Georgia, Texas, Virginia, Arkansas, and Tennessee.

After the Civil War, thousands of newly freed slaves left Louisiana and other southern states.

When the war ended in 1865, Louisiana's economy had collapsed. Many people, broke and shattered by the war, left Louisiana for good, becoming pioneers in the West. Thousands of newly freed slaves headed west or to northern cities to find work and a new life in freedom. Louisianans who stayed faced the huge task of rebuilding their state.

NEW LAWS AND NEW PROBLEMS

When the Civil War ended, the freed slaves still had no rights or land. Most could not find work. Louisiana politicians passed laws similar to the slavery laws prior to the war, severely restricting African Americans' freedoms.

In 1868, the U.S. Congress passed constitutional amendments granting freedom and equality to African Americans. That same year, Louisiana's state government followed suit by creating a new state constitution. Although the state's legislature had white majorities, particularly in the senate, the constitutional aconvention had 49 white and 49 black delegates. In 1872, P. B. S. Pinchback was elected governor of Louisiana, making him the first black governor of any state. Among other things, the new constitution gave voting rights to black men, established a free public school system, and guaranteed blacks equal access to public facilities.

At first, blacks were glad to use these new freedoms. But their happiness soon turned sour because the government rarely enforced the new laws. African Americans still faced the same **discrimination** they had during the time of slavery. Riots and election fraud restored white power. Racist groups such as the Ku Klux Klan (KKK) attacked and terrorized blacks and their white supporters. In 1876, the KKK carried out violent raids against black civilians to scare them away from voting. The northern states and federal government did nothing to help.

THE ROAD TO RECOVERY

The process of reorganizing the government after the war was long. In 1877, **Reconstruction** officially ended in Louisiana. The state remained mostly agricultural, but the huge plantations were replaced with small farms and **sharecroppers**. New Orleans declined as a trading city because fewer steamboats and trade ships made port there. These ports, once so vital to commerce, were now bypassed by the new, faster networks of railroads that crisscrossed the coun-

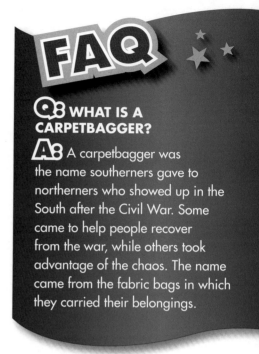

FAQ

Q8 WHAT IS A CARPETBAGGER?

A8 A carpetbagger was the name southerners gave to northerners who showed up in the South after the Civil War. Some came to help people recover from the war, while others took advantage of the chaos. The name came from the fabric bags in which they carried their belongings.

WORDS TO KNOW

discrimination *the unfair treatment of a group, based on its race, age, gender, or other characteristic*

Reconstruction *the period after the Civil War when the Southern states were reorganized and reestablished in the Union*

sharecroppers *farmers who give a portion of their crops as rent for the land*

MINI-BIO

JOHN WILLIS MENARD: GROUNDBREAKING POLITICIAN

John Willis Menard (1838–1893) was born in the Free State of Illinois. After the Civil War, he moved to New Orleans and became active in city government. He also published a newspaper. In 1868, Menard became the first person of color to be elected to the U.S. Congress when he was chosen to fill a vacant house seat. But his opponent contested the election, and Congress refused to grant him his seat. However, he gave a speech in the House of Representatives— becoming the first black man to do so.

? Want to know more? Visit www.factsfornow .scholastic.com and enter the keyword **Louisiana**.

WORDS TO KNOW

Jim Crow laws *laws that were passed to enforce racial segregation and to prevent African Americans from doing things that white people could do*

segregated *the forced separation of one group from the rest of society*

civil rights *basic rights that are guaranteed to all citizens*

try. Louisiana was no longer the center of cotton or sugarcane production, so the once-huge shipments of sugar and cotton that sailed from New Orleans to foreign countries no longer existed.

Recovery in the late 1800s was very slow. After the first gains toward equal rights, politicians opposed to equality took control of the Louisiana government. These men included deeply racist former plantation owners and wealthy New Orleans businessmen. The lawmakers passed **Jim Crow laws** that discriminated against people of color, and **segregated** schools and public places. Through nonviolent protests, African Americans were able to gain the right to ride on the horse-drawn streetcars of New Orleans. But it would be decades before blacks in Louisiana would be given their **civil rights**.

BIG INDUSTRY

In the late 1800s, northern lumber companies became very interested in harvesting the vast yellow pine forests that covered Louisiana. By 1888, Louisiana had sold almost 2 million acres (800,000 ha) of forestland to northern timber companies. The companies built sawmills and employed thousands of Louisianans. In 1914, Louisiana ranked first in the country in lumber production. Once

the companies finished clear-cutting many of the forests, they packed up and left, leaving miles of destroyed acreage and hundreds of unemployed workers.

Several other industries brought renewed hope to Louisiana's recovery. Oil and natural gas were discovered in Louisiana in the early part of the 20th century. Sulfur was discovered, and the first sulfur mine opened in 1909. Salt mines sprang up on Avery Island, where the biggest salt deposits were found. Today, Louisiana still ranks number one in the country in salt production. As the new century dawned, Louisiana had hope, but many challenges ahead.

These longleaf pine logs were loaded onto a horse-drawn cart that took them to a factory for processing in 1904.

Avery Island's salt mine is the oldest salt mine in the Western Hemisphere. It produces 10,000 tons of salt every day.

READ ABOUT

This steamboat
carries bales of
cotton on the
Mississippi River
near Baton Rouge.

▲ **1928**
*Huey P. Long
becomes governor*

1956 ▲
*The Lake Pontchartrain
Causeway is completed*

1960
*Public schools in New
Orleans are desegregated*

CHAPTER FIVE

MORE MODERN TIMES

★

D URING WORLD WAR I, LOUISIANA FARMERS BENEFITED FROM HIGHER PRICES FOR COTTON, WHICH WAS USED FOR WAR SUPPLIES. But the windfall didn't last. Once the war ended, prices fell. Louisiana's fortunes changed with the 1928 election of Huey P. Long as governor.

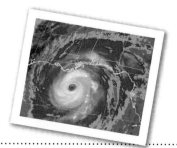

1977

Ernest "Dutch" Morial is elected the first black mayor of New Orleans

2005 ▲

Hurricanes Katrina and Rita hit southern Louisiana

2010

A massive oil spill causes damage to the Louisiana coast

GOVERNOR HUEY P. LONG

Long was born poor and became incredibly popular with working-class Louisianans. He proclaimed "Every man a king, but no one wears a crown," and people believed him. Long fought against big corporations that took advantage of ordinary citizens. He represented a change from the plantation owner to that of the working person and rural farmer.

Long instituted sweeping changes. He paved roads, improved schools in both white and black districts, and helped poor people by giving free textbooks to children, eliminating some taxes, and creating thousands of jobs. Over the years, some people criticized the way Long tried to control the government and how he handled the state's money. But in 1930, he was elected to the U.S. Senate and continued to work for Louisianans, building highways, bridges, and schools. He supported free medical care for the poor and worked to make Louisiana universities, such as Louisiana State University, among the best in the country.

Long had ambitions of being president of the United States, but he would never get the opportunity. On September 8, 1935, he was shot on the steps of the Louisiana Capitol and died two days later. Reportedly, his last words were, "God, don't let me die. I have so much to do."

Huey P. Long speaks at a campaign rally.

THE GREAT DEPRESSION AND WORLD WAR II

In 1929, the year after Long was elected governor, the United States plunged deeper into a financial crisis known as the Great Depression. The stock market crashed, and thousands of Americans were suddenly out of work. But Long created jobs for Louisianans on public projects such as road building, school construction, and flood-control projects. He taxed the wealthy and used the money to help the poor. He bribed and threatened legislators to approve his measures. "I used to get things done by saying please," Long once said. "Now I dynamite them out of my path." President Franklin Delano Roosevelt compared him to a dictator.

During World War II (1939–1945), Louisiana oil and gas companies provided fuel to America's European allies. Factories and businesses in large Louisiana towns employed thousands of workers. The economic depression began to lift. In 1941, the Japanese military bombed the U.S. naval base at Pearl Harbor, Hawaii. This attack led to the United States finally entering the war.

During the Great Depression, these chair makers lived out of their car in Paradise, Louisiana.

SHOES

RATIONING BOARD

WAR BOOK 2   WAR BOOK I

RATIONING BOARD
GASOLINE   TIRES

America's short supply of resources forced citizens to ration everything from food to shoes and gasoline. Here people in New Orleans wait to enter a local rationing board.

At home, Louisianans contributed to the war effort. While many men became soldiers, women were encouraged to work outside the home in factories and other professions that once had been closed to them. Families endured rationing, which imposed strict limits on everything from food and clothing to supplies such as rubber and gasoline. Families planted fruits and vegetables in their own "victory gardens."

At the end of the war, the economy continued to be strong. For the first time, more Louisianans worked in cities than on farms. New industries came to the state. Oil refineries and other big manufacturers created new

jobs. Louisiana was on the verge of great economic prosperity and social change.

CHANGES IN LOUISIANA

Throughout the 20th century, African Americans struggled for civil rights. In the 1950s, these efforts slowly began to pay off. In 1954, in the landmark case *Brown v. Board of Education*, the U.S. Supreme Court put an end to legal segregation in public schools. Still, the state government attempted to fight school integration. But some in Louisiana defied these attempts.

In 1960, in New Orleans, six-year-old Ruby Bridges became the first black child in the United States to attend an all-white school. Her classmates threatened and harassed her, and her father and grandparents lost their jobs. But she and other African Americans stood up for their rights.

By the next school year, Louisiana schools were desegregated. The old Jim Crow laws—which maintained that African Americans had "separate but equal" opportunities to those of whites—were changed, and African Americans finally had access to the same public places as whites. Over the next decades, African Americans gained more political and economic strength.

In the 1960s, Louisiana's population grew from 3.26 million to 3.64 million people. However, African

RUBY BRIDGES: BREAKING BARRIERS

Ruby Bridges (1954–) did something remarkably brave on November 14, 1960. She became the first African American student to attend a white school in New Orleans. From that day on, Ruby walked past screaming mobs and into her classroom, where she was the only black student. By the time she started second grade, her school was integrated. After graduating from high school and attending business school, she became a travel agent. In 1999, she created the Ruby Bridges Foundation, which teaches tolerance and respect for people of all races. She also wrote a children's book about her experiences.

? Want to know more? Visit www.factsfornow .scholastic.com. Enter the keyword **Louisiana** and look for the Biography logo.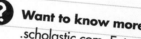

THE LONGEST BRIDGE IN THE WORLD

People had long tried to figure out a fast way across Lake Pontchartrain. But it took a new technology to make it happen. Prestressed concrete is extremely strong and perfect for building large structures such as bridges. Workers began construction on May 23, 1955, and the bridge opened on August 30, 1956, with a huge celebration.

To this day, the causeway is the longest over-water highway in the world. The 24-mile-long (39 km) bridge stretches across the lake, linking Metairie and Mandeville, Louisiana. More than 42,000 vehicles cross the bridge every day.

When the Lake Pontchartrain Causeway opened in 1956, it was an engineering wonder.

Americans left Louisiana by the thousands, both because of discrimination and for better job opportunities in northern cities. Farming continued to decline, mainly because small-scale farmers couldn't compete with the large agricultural businesses that arose after World War II. Many farm families sold their properties to the farming corporations and left.

Education made great advances in the 1960s. The illiteracy rate in the state dropped dramatically, and enrollment boomed at Louisiana colleges.

During the 1970s, Louisiana went through many significant changes, not the least of which was a new recognition of women's rights. In 1974, the Louisiana legislature created a new state constitution that included equal-rights provisions. Three years later, Ernest "Dutch" Morial was elected as the first African American mayor of New Orleans.

The 1970s were boom years for the Louisiana economy, as well. Rising oil and gas prices throughout the world brought great prosperity to the state. People flocked to good-paying jobs at refineries and chemical companies. Many people made more money, and some could afford luxuries they had never before enjoyed. Louisiana's economic boom and low labor costs drew many businesses and industries.

CHALLENGES AHEAD

In the 1980s, oil prices fell dramatically around the world, throwing Louisiana into a statewide economic depression. One idea to bring money into the state was the legalization of gambling. Casinos opened and succeeded, especially those near the Texas border and in New Orleans.

Visitors in a horse-drawn carriage taking a tour of New Orleans

Tourism grew in the 1980s, becoming one of Louisiana's biggest industries. People from all over the world came to stroll through the streets of New Orleans, sample spicy Cajun and Creole foods, and visit the old plantation homes. Parks, cultural events, and the yearly Mardi Gras festival in New Orleans also attracted tourists and visitors.

But the state faced great challenges in the 1990s. Population growth remained sluggish, with

After Hurricane Katrina, waters quickly rose, as high as 15 feet (5 m), and flooded 80 percent of New Orleans.

only a small increase in the number of people moving to the state. Despite more jobs, more people lived in poverty than in any other state. Low-paying jobs, a lack of opportunity, and a struggling educational system continued to plague residents. Louisiana continued to grapple with ongoing racial issues. Environmental damage from oil refineries and other petroleum-based industries brought further challenges.

On August 29, 2005, Hurricane Katrina pounded the Gulf Coast, destroying parts of Louisiana, including most neighborhoods in New Orleans. When the storm surges breached, or broke through, several levees in New Orleans, it caused catastrophic flooding in more than 80 percent of the city.

Despite Louisiana's history with devastating hurricanes, the state and federal governments had failed to prepare proper evacuation procedures. Many people did not survive. Tens of thousands more crammed into the Superdome, a sports arena in New Orleans, living in terrible conditions, with nothing to eat or drink for more than a week. Government assistance was slow to arrive.

The total number of deaths from Katrina was 1,836, and 1,577 of those were in Louisiana. Entire towns were virtually wiped out. Hundreds of thousands of homes and businesses were lost. Schools and hospitals were severely damaged or destroyed. Oil rigs in the Gulf were destroyed. Thousands of Katrina evacuees fled to other cities. Problems with homeowners collecting

Lasting Effects

THINK ABOUT IT!

A medical study released in 2013 shows that current New Orleans residents have a three-times greater risk of heart attack than New Orleans residents did prior to Hurricane Katrina. Doctors studied heart attack patients in the six years after Katrina. They compared them to heart attack patients who were treated before the hurricane. The doctors discovered that post-Katrina residents were less likely to take their medicines. They were also more likely to smoke, drink alcohol heavily, and have higher levels of stress and mental illness. The post-Katrina group was more likely to be out of work and without health insurance. These factors made it more difficult for them to receive effective treatment. Researchers concluded that large-scale disasters such as Katrina affect the behavior of a population and its medical needs. "The massive devastation of Hurricane Katrina has broken the infrastructure of New Orleans, and its effects are much more far-reaching than we expected," said Dr. Anand Irimpen, senior investigator of the study.

Source: *Medical Daily*, March 7, 2013

Many New Orleans residents lost their homes in Hurricane Katrina. Here, displaced people wait for buses to take them to shelter in Houston, Texas, on September 1, 2005.

insurance and the high cost of rebuilding made returning to Louisiana impossible for many economically disadvantaged evacuees. By July 2006, the population of New Orleans had decreased by about 225,000 people.

In June 2006, the U.S. Army Corps of Engineers, which oversees the construction and maintenance of the levees, officially took responsibility for the levee failures during Katrina. Over the following years, the levees were rebuilt with improved design and construction in order to avoid future levee failures.

TOWARD A BRIGHTER FUTURE

The people of Louisiana are still rebuilding in the aftermath of Katrina, but the future is looking brighter each day. Although many residents left New Orleans for good, others are returning in large numbers. The population of New Orleans grew by 2 percent between 2011 and 2012. As the population increases, new business opportunities are being created. Engineering and construction have grown considerably. Tax monies collected by the city are also rising, which means New Orleans can provide better health, education, and transportation services to residents.

As residents continued their post-Katrina recovery, another disaster struck Louisiana. In April 2010, an underwater oil-drilling rig called the *Deepwater Horizon* exploded 41 miles (66 km) off the coast. For three months, oil gushed nonstop from the ocean floor into the Gulf of Mexico. The oil killed millions of fish, birds, and other wildlife. It reached Louisiana's shores and devastated the fishing and tourism industries.

Recovery from the oil spill and Hurricane Katrina will take years to complete. But Louisianans are resilient and hopeful. There are big challenges ahead, but Louisianans will face them the same way they've faced things in the past: with determination and hard work.

Workers at the rebuilding site of a levee in New Orleans

READ ABOUT

A huge crowd fills the French Quarter in New Orleans for Mardi Gras 2011.

CHAPTER SIX

PEOPLE

★

LOUISIANA'S PEOPLE REFLECT A RICH MIX OF CULTURES, RELIGIONS, TRADITIONS, AND NATIONALITIES. Before Europeans arrived, the Native peoples of Louisiana helped one another. Spaniards, French, Africans, and Native Americans lived side by side for years. As different people have come into the state, they have brought new celebrations and traditions to the cultural mix. Today, many Louisianans trace their family roots not only to other countries, but to specific places in Louisiana where their ancestors first settled.

A CULTURAL GUMBO

By the beginning of the 19th century, disease, war, and slavery had destroyed the Indian way of life. But the Native Americans were survivors. By the 20th century, several Indian groups had begun to recover. Today, they host powwows and events throughout the state, sharing and celebrating their heritage and their history. Some Native American groups own successful casinos and other businesses.

Early French and Spanish settlers and African slaves left distinctive marks on New Orleans's architecture, food, and society. In the 19th and 20th centuries, Italian, German, Jewish, and Irish immigrants brought their unique influences to New Orleans. In recent years, many others—including Latinos from the Caribbean and Central and South America, Greeks, Haitians, Filipinos, and Asians—have moved to New Orleans and added new "flavors" to the city's multicultural mix.

From the beginning of Louisiana's history, people from all over the world settled among the bayous and remained fairly rural and remote from the rest of Louisiana. Some families in the southern areas are descended from English-speaking plantation owners and other white landowners. French-speaking Creoles settled in the southwestern Louisiana prairie lands.

People QuickFacts

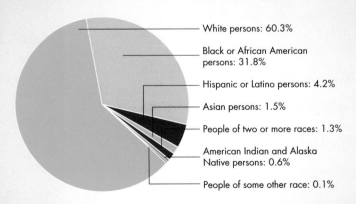

White persons: 60.3%

Black or African American persons: 31.8%

Hispanic or Latino persons: 4.2%

Asian persons: 1.5%

People of two or more races: 1.3%

American Indian and Alaska Native persons: 0.6%

People of some other race: 0.1%

Source: U.S. Census Bureau, 2010 census

THE CAJUN AND CREOLE CULTURES

Two Louisiana cultures you won't find anywhere else are the Cajun and the Creole, with a strong base in New Orleans. The Cajuns, or Acadians, were originally a group of French settlers in Canada in the 1600s. In the mid-1700s, the British forced them out of Canada, and many of them settled in rural Louisiana. Cajuns are proud of their French roots. Their language is a mix of French, African, and English. Foods such as gumbo, celebrations such as the *fais do-do* (dance), and traditions such as eating gumbo at Christmas dinner all are deeply embedded in New Orleans culture. *Creole,* as used in New Orleans, refers to people of mixed French, Spanish, and African heritage, who are native to Louisiana.

The Islenos have created a unique culture in south Louisiana. Islenos are descended from Canary Islanders who settled the area in the 1760s. Today, Islenos live in small communities and have kept their unique Spanish dialect.

A Cajun man prepares Cajun-style Louisiana crawfish.

Big City Life

This list shows the population of Louisiana's biggest cities.

New Orleans	343,829
Baton Rouge	229,493
Shreveport	199,311
Lafayette	120,623
Lake Charles	71,993
Kenner	66,702

Source: U.S. Census Bureau, 2010 census

TOWNS AND CITIES

As you travel north from New Orleans, society changes dramatically. Some have described north Louisiana as a patchwork quilt, with each piece remaining intact and coexisting side by side. Throughout this region, both blacks and whites live in urban cities and rural communities.

Where Louisianans Live

The colors on this map indicate population density throughout the state. The darker the color, the more people live there.

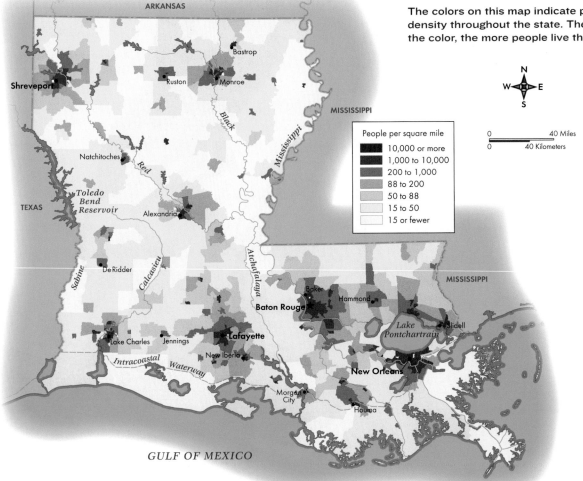

Since before the Civil War, Louisiana has been primarily a rural state. In fact, vast numbers of Louisianans live in small towns and cities with fewer than 100,000 people.

GETTING AROUND IN NEW ORLEANS

One question that people always ask is, "How do people in Louisiana get around?" Actually, in New Orleans, everyone loves taking the Saint Charles rail streetcar line. Distinctly southern, and distinctly New Orleans, the streetcar system has been active for a very long time and stands as a symbol of New Orleans style.

The Saint Charles streetcar line in New Orleans and the San Francisco, California, cable cars are the nation's only mobile national monuments!

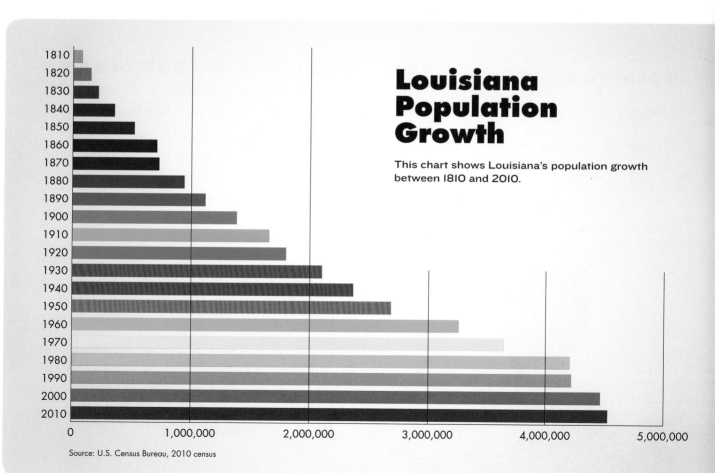

Louisiana Population Growth

This chart shows Louisiana's population growth between 1810 and 2010.

Source: U.S. Census Bureau, 2010 census

HOW TO TALK LIKE A LOUISIANAN

With their mix of French words, southern phrases, and just plain one-of-a-kindness, Cajuns in Louisiana talk like no one else. Here are some examples:

- Make a bill: buy groceries
- Ma chagren: I'm sorry
- My eye! (or My foot!): no way!
- Go to bed!: I don't believe you
- Make the veiller (vey-yea): stay up all night talking with friends
- Slow the TV: turn down the volume
- Speed up the TV: turn up the volume
- Meenoo: cat

WORDS TO KNOW

bisque *a rich, creamy soup*

étouffée *a spicy, Cajun-style stew served over rice*

Louisiana chef Paul Prudhomme

HOW TO EAT LIKE A LOUISIANAN

What's the most distinctive thing about Louisiana? Its food! Food in Louisiana is savored, discussed, argued over, and shared constantly.

Over the years, Louisiana cooking has borrowed from the food traditions of many world cultures to create a unique flavor. Many of the rich sauces and stewed foods, such as **bisque** and **étouffée**, and breads such as beignets (square doughnuts coated with powdered sugar) and *corasse* (fried bread dough with syrup) come from French cuisine. Louisianans got spicy jambalaya (a rice dish) from the Spanish.

African influences on Louisiana cuisine include okra, barbecue, and deep-fat frying. Caribbean influences can be seen in many bean and rice dishes, such as rice and congri (crowder peas and rice). Cornbread and filé (a spice) came from Native Americans.

MENU

WHAT'S ON THE MENU IN LOUISIANA?

★ ★ ★

Andouille (ahn-do-ee)
A hard, smoked, highly seasoned pork sausage found in many Louisiana dishes, such as gumbo.

Boudin (boo-dan)
Ground pork mixed with onions and rice and stuffed into sausage casings. Some people like them hot, spicy, and dry. Others say that mild and juicy is the only way to go.

Crawfish
Known as mudbugs, sweet-tasting crawfish are baked, boiled, fried, steamed, and put into every dish imaginable.

Gumbo
No food says "Louisiana" like gumbo. Basically, gumbo is a soup with two or more meats, served with rice. But it's more than that—it's history in a bowl! The word *gumbo* comes from *nkombo*, a Bantu African word for okra.

Muffuletta
This Louisiana sandwich is a huge pile of meats, cheeses, and olive salad stuffed between two plate-sized slabs of Italian bread.

Gumbo

TRY THIS RECIPE
Pralines
You haven't had a true New Orleans treat until you've popped a praline in your mouth. This sweet candy patty is made from sugar, butter, water, and pecans. Try this simple recipe at home. Be sure to ask an adult to help you.

Pralines

Ingredients:
1 cup light brown sugar, packed
1 cup granulated sugar
½ cup light cream
1½ cups pecans, halved
2 tablespoons butter

Instructions:
1. Combine the sugars with the cream in a saucepan and cook over medium heat, stirring occasionally with a wooden spoon, until the mixture forms a thick syrup.
2. Add the pecans and butter and continue to cook over medium heat, stirring frequently until all the pecans are thoroughly coated.
3. Remove from the heat and let cool for 10 minutes.
4. Use a spoon to drop rounded balls of the mixture onto a sheet of waxed paper or aluminum foil, leaving space between each ball for the pralines to spread. Allow to cool. Makes about 12 candies.

LOUIS ARMSTRONG: THE GREAT SATCHMO

Born in New Orleans, jazz legend Louis Armstrong (1901–1971) learned to play the cornet as a boy. Later, he played with pickup bands in clubs and on the streets, and his raw talent caught the attention of older experienced musicians. Soon he was performing with professional bands and on Mississippi riverboats.

In 1922, Armstrong joined "King" Joe Oliver's band at Chicago's famous Royal Garden nightclub. Each night, the Savannah Syncopators' New Orleans sound thrilled hundreds of young people of every race. Jazz soon swept into Kansas City and New York and then moved overseas to capture England, France, and Japan. In a few years, Armstrong was so popular he got his own band and was invited to tour European cities.

? Want to know more? Visit www.factsfornow .scholastic.com and enter the keyword **Louisiana**.

MUSIC AND ALL THAT JAZZ

From the rip-roaring riffs of jazz to the foot-tapping sounds of zydeco and Cajun, or the deep, melancholy tones of the blues—there's nothing that's more American, and Louisianan, than these music forms.

Jazz has been called America's Music because it was created by so many different cultures joining their musical styles into something fresh and new. Africans, Creoles, Italians, Germans, and Irish mingled together to make the raucous, free-form jazz sound that Louisiana is famous for.

Other musical styles fill Louisiana. The Cajuns brought their fiddles and their distinctive sound

Dr. John performs at the 2013 New Orleans Jazz and Heritage Festival.

to Louisiana when they arrived from Canada. Germans introduced the accordion to the Cajuns, and now that instrument has become key to the sound of Cajun music. Later, Africans added a scratchy washboard beat to Cajun music and created zydeco, a combination of traditional Cajun dance music, a little rhythm and blues, and African music. Latin salsa is another form of music that can be heard in Louisiana clubs.

Louisiana's rich musical heritage has bred several world-class performers. Lil Wayne is a popular New Orleans–born rapper. *American Idol* judge Randy Jackson was born in Baton Rouge. Composer and singer Randy Newman was born in New Orleans and has created music for many well-known movies. Singer Aaron Neville hails from New Orleans. He and his brothers Art, Charles, and Cyril (and son Ivan) make up the Neville Brothers, a band that plays R & B, soul, and jazz.

Cajun musician Rosie Ledet performs at the New Orleans Jazz and Heritage Festival in April 2005.

BUDDY GUY: THE KING OF BLUES GUITAR

Buddy Guy (1936–) was born and raised in Lettsworth, where he taught himself the guitar at an early age. In the early 1950s, he began performing blues music with bands in Baton Rouge. In 1957, he moved to Chicago, Illinois, where he became a popular guitarist in the city's thriving blues scene. Guy played on numerous recordings by blues legends Muddy Waters, Howlin' Wolf, Koko Taylor, and others. Many rock guitarists, including Jimi Hendrix, Eric Clapton, and Stevie Ray Vaughan, were influenced by his flashy style. Guy has won six Grammy Awards and the National Medal of Arts, awarded by President George W. Bush in 2003.

? Want to know more? Visit www.factsfornow.scholastic.com and enter the keyword **Louisiana**.

MAKING MUSIC

In the Delta region, music born from the torment and anguish of slavery and discrimination gave many African Americans a voice. As early as 1895, black musicians such as Buddy Bolden formed bands that played unrehearsed, improvised music to a fast beat or slow blues. Most of these musicians could not read music (and many could not read at all), but their horns could sing this new and exciting "New Orleans Jazz."

COLEEN SALLEY: TELLING STORIES

Anyone who loves picture books has probably heard of Coleen Salley (1929–2008) and her Epossumondas books. But she wasn't always a writer. In fact, Salley didn't publish her first book until she was 72 years old! Before that, she had a career as a professor at the University of New Orleans. Later, she became a storyteller and writer, touring the world and telling stories. Her children's books include Why Epossumondas Has No Hair on His Tail and Who's That Tripping Over My Bridge? Until her death in 2008, she presided as Queen Coleen over her very own parade float each year at Mardi Gras.

? Want to know more? Visit www.factsfornow .scholastic.com and enter the keyword **Louisiana**.

Louisiana native Ellen DeGeneres is a popular TV talk show host.

ART AND CULTURE

Novelist Shirley Ann Grau was born in New Orleans, and much of her writing is set in the South. She won the Pulitzer Prize in 1965 for *The Keepers of the House.*

Ellen DeGeneres was the voice of Dory in *Finding Nemo.* Born in Metairie, a suburb of New Orleans, she's also a comedian, actor, and TV personality. Actor Faith Ford was born in Alexandria and raised in Pineville.

The television series *Treme* followed a group of characters living in New Orleans in the aftermath of Hurricane Katrina. It featured many local actors and performances from real-life New Orleans musicians.

Brothers Greg and Bryant Gumbel were both born in New Orleans. Greg is a sportscaster who became the first person of color to do the play-by-play of a major U.S. sports championship when he called the Super Bowl in 2001. Bryant cohosted the *Today Show* for years and is currently a news and sports journalist. Author and journalist Cokie Roberts is a well-respected correspondent for National Public Radio (NPR). She was born in New Orleans.

Parade watchers on Canal Street in New Orleans reach out for beads being thrown from the Jester float.

LET THE GOOD TIMES ROLL!

In Louisiana, you'll hear the French expression *Laissez le bon temps rouler* (less-say lay bon tonh roo-lay), or "Let the good times roll!" That's the motto of many Louisianans, who love parties and celebrations as much as they love good food.

The biggest festival is, hands down, Mardi Gras, held in February or March. Mardi Gras is also the Tuesday before Lent. Lent is a 40-day period of prayer and reflection, recognized by many Christians, that begins on Ash Wednesday and ends on Easter Sunday. So Mardi Gras, which means "fat Tuesday," is the last day to party hard—and Louisiana does! There are Mardi Gras celebrations throughout the state, but the biggest one is in New Orleans. For the two weeks leading up

NEWCOMB POTTERY

In 1894, the faculty of H. Sophie Newcomb Memorial College (now part of Tulane University in New Orleans) had what was considered to be a radical idea: To combine teaching a practical trade to women with training in the fine arts. The result was a commercial art studio whose stunning ceramics were in demand for more than 40 years.

Newcomb Pottery produced more than 70,000 pieces designed by approximately 90 women artists. Women were always the designers; men were always the potters. But Newcomb wasn't a factory. It was an artists' studio. Each piece was one-of-a-kind, made by hand and decorated with natural motifs, such as trees and animals. These motifs, as well as the beautiful colors and glazes, made Newcomb pottery famous.

The studio closed in 1940, but at the Newcomb Art Gallery on the campus of Tulane University, you can see many examples of early Newcomb Pottery.

to Ash Wednesday, parades fill the streets at night. Organizations called "krewes" build huge, elaborate floats, which they ride in the parade, wearing costumes and throwing plastic necklaces and trinkets to the roaring crowds. Millions of visitors stroll the streets, listening to music spilling out of restaurants and clubs.

Mardi Gras isn't the only Louisiana festival. Music festivals are held throughout the year, celebrating jazz, blues, bluegrass, and Cajun music. Food festivals devoted entirely to specific dishes—such as gumbo, étouffée, oysters, catfish, crawfish, and strawberries—keep Louisianans eating well all year long. Native Americans celebrate their heritages with powwows.

EDUCATION IN LOUISIANA

In the 1960s and 1970s, the civil rights movement opened Louisiana public schools to all children, and the state made a commitment to educating them. New schools were built, and there was a sense of excitement in education. The oil boom of the 1970s kept money flowing into the state, and educational opportunities flourished.

But amid the excitement were signs that Louisiana's education wasn't as healthy as it could have been. Educators realized that there was work to be done. Schools tried to reduce class sizes and get students and teachers the resources they needed.

Today, more than 80 percent of New Orleans students attend charter schools, or schools that receive public funding and operate privately. The rest attend schools operated by a state-run agency. Results of the new system are encouraging. Before Katrina, only 35 percent of New Orleans's public school students passed state tests. Today, that figure is 60 percent.

GREETINGS FROM LOUISIANA STATE UNIVERSITY

CAMPANILE, LOUISIANA STATE UNIVERSITY BATON ROUGE, LA.

© CURT TEICH & CO., INC.

98-H1859

Louisiana State University can trace its origin to the early 1800s. This postcard dates to 1949.

Educators hope that each year will bring more students and more schools back to New Orleans. Looking to the future, educators envision a smaller school system with more opportunities for everyone. In the short term, however, educators are doing the best they can to rebuild the city's school system.

Louisiana is home to a number of outstanding institutions of higher education. Louisiana State University (LSU) is a jewel in the state's education system. Founded in 1860 as the Louisiana State Seminary and Military Academy, today LSU enrolls 30,000 students in its undergraduate and graduate programs. The campus consists of more than 250 attractive buildings constructed in different architectural styles. Tulane, a private university located in New Orleans, was founded in 1834, and has a total enrollment of 13,500 students.

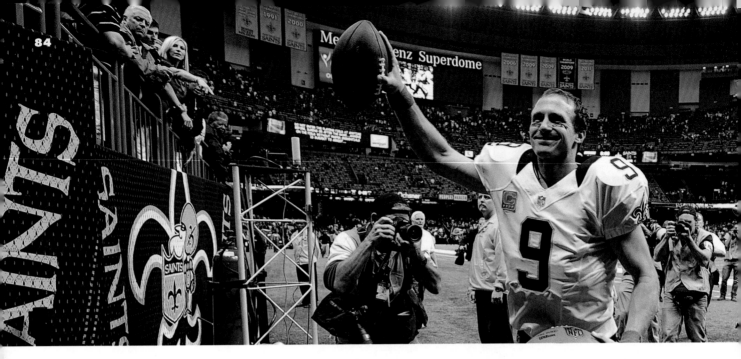

The New Orleans Saints are the pride of the city. Here, quarterback Drew Brees celebrates a 2012 win over the San Diego Chargers.

LOUISIANA AT PLAY

Are you ready for some football? Lots of people in Louisiana are. The National Football League's New Orleans Saints have been a top team for years. In the 2006–2007 season, they won the nation's hearts as they reached the postseason playoffs. They eventually lost to the Chicago Bears and missed a chance at the Super Bowl. However, the Saints came roaring back to win the Super Bowl in the 2009–2010 season. In post-Katrina Louisiana, the Saints gave people reason to be hopeful and excited by a true Cinderella story.

The Mannings are a Louisiana football family. Archie Manning was quarterback for the New Orleans Saints from 1971 to 1982. His sons have become NFL quarterbacks, too. Eli has led the New York Giants to two Super Bowl victories and was named Super Bowl MVP both times. Peyton led the Indianapolis Colts to victory in the 2007 Super Bowl, earning him the MVP award. All of them were born in Louisiana.

At the college level, LSU and Louisiana Tech have powerhouse athletic teams. In 2007, the LSU football team won the Sugar Bowl, one of college football's top events. In 2009, the university's men's basketball team won its 11th Southeastern Conference championship, and the women's track-and-field team has won many national championships. LSU's baseball team has won six national championships.

Louisiana is also home to pro basketball's New Orleans Pelicans. This team originated in Charlotte, North Carolina, and moved to Louisiana in 2002. After Hurricane Katrina, the team played temporarily in Oklahoma while its stadium was repaired.

Gymnast Carly Patterson

A basketball great with a history in Louisiana was "Pistol" Pete Maravich. Born in Pennsylvania, he played basketball at LSU in Baton Rouge. He scored more points in college than any other player in history. He later played professional basketball for the Atlanta Hawks, the New Orleans Jazz, the Utah Jazz (after the team moved), and the Boston Celtics. The LSU home court is now known as the Pete Maravich Assembly Center.

But the state isn't just about football or basketball. Carly Patterson, a gymnast who won three Olympic medals at the 2004 Summer Games, was born in New Orleans. David Toms is a professional golfer who was born in Monroe and now makes his home in Shreveport. He won the 2001 PGA Championship. Athletes and artists, songwriters and educators—they're all proud to call Louisiana home.

READ ABOUT

Louisiana's Old
State House was
renovated in the
1990s and now
houses a museum.

CHAPTER SEVEN

GOVERNMENT

★

IN 1847, THE CITY OF BATON ROUGE DONATED A PIECE OF LAND FOR THE STATE CAPITOL. And what a piece of land it was! Located high on a bluff, it overlooked the Mississippi River. Only the most magnificent building was worthy of such a spot, so the people of Baton Rouge built the grandest structure ever seen in Louisiana.

Capitol Facts

The state's government is housed in the Louisiana State Capitol, a building that was the dream of Governor Huey P. Long. He orchestrated its construction, but it was not in use until the inauguration of his successor, Oscar K. Allen. It has a classical design with art deco details and is the tallest building in Louisiana.

Here are some fascinating facts about Louisiana's state capitol:

Exterior height . . . . 450 feet (137 m)
Number of floors 34
Surrounding park . . .Former grounds of Louisiana State University
Location . . . . . . North 3rd Street and Capital Drive, Baton Rouge
Construction dates 1930–1932
Cost of construction . . . . $5 million

WOW

At 450 feet (137 m), Louisiana's capitol is the tallest in the United States.

Louisiana's State Capitol

HISTORIC BUILDING

The building looked like a castle, with towers, turrets, and stained-glass windows that reminded visitors of a great medieval cathedral. But some people didn't like it at all. Mark Twain called it the ugliest building on the Mississippi River.

During the Civil War, Union troops used the building as a prison and a military post for African American troops. It caught fire twice, and after the war was over, the Union abandoned the burned-out shell of a building. By 1882, it was reconstructed, and the refurbished statehouse remained in use until 1932, when it was abandoned for Huey P. Long's new building. Today, the Old State House is a museum.

Capital City

This map shows places of interest in Baton Rouge, Louisiana's state capital.

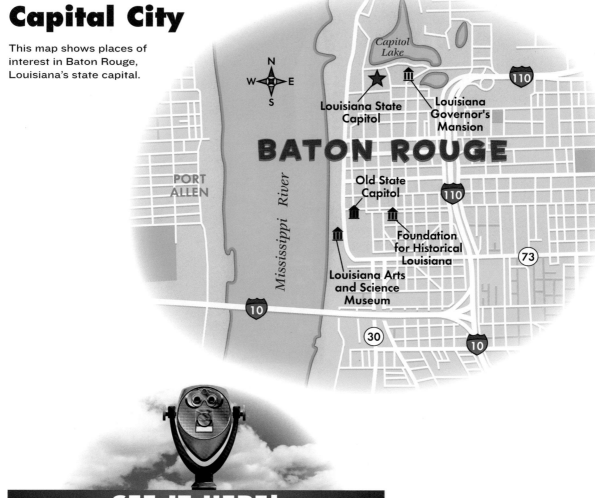

SEE IT HERE!

LOUISIANA STATE CAPITOL

You can't miss it—the tall, elegant building in Baton Rouge. The Louisiana state capitol is a symbol of pride and celebration for the entire state.

The limestone and marble used to build it came from as far away as Italy. The entire building is decorated with images of the brown pelican, the state bird.

Louisiana art abounds throughout the capitol. In the Memorial Hall, a large bronze map shows the state and its parishes. Murals show scenes of family, the harvest, farmlands, and the arts. Enormous bronze doors, each weighing a ton, open into each chamber of the capitol.

Governor Bobby Jindal addresses a joint session of the Louisiana legislature in the state capitol.

JAMES CARVILLE: THE RAGIN' CAJUN

Like him or not, no one can deny that James Carville (1944–) has had a powerful impact on American politics. Carville was born and raised in Carville! He graduated from Louisiana State University, became a lawyer, and served in the U.S. Marine Corps for two years. In the 1980s, he worked as a political consultant, helping politicians win elections. In 1992, he was part of the consulting team that helped Bill Clinton win the U.S. presidency. Today, Carville is a political and sports commentator on television.

? Want to know more? Visit www. factsfornow .scholastic.com. Enter the keyword **Louisiana** and look for the Biography logo.

RUNNING THE STATE

In order to run a diverse, lively, and unique state such as Louisiana, a firm, stable, and effective government must be in place. Like other states modeled after the U.S. federal government, Louisiana has three branches of government committed to keeping the state strong. Each of these branches has specific duties. They work with one another to make sure that no one branch gets too much power. That's called the system of checks and balances.

Louisiana's State Government

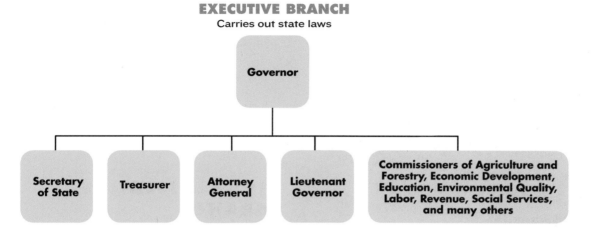

EXECUTIVE BRANCH
Carries out state laws

Governor

Secretary of State

Treasurer

Attorney General

Lieutenant Governor

Commissioners of Agriculture and Forestry, Economic Development, Education, Environmental Quality, Labor, Revenue, Social Services, and many others

LEGISLATIVE BRANCH
Makes and passes state laws

Senate (39 members)

House of Representatives (105 members)

JUDICIAL BRANCH
Enforces state laws

State Supreme Court

Appeals Court (5 circuits)

District Court (40 districts with 64 parishes)

THE EXECUTIVE BRANCH

The first of Louisiana's three branches of government is the executive branch. The governor leads this branch. The governor is responsible for administering all the laws passed by the legislature. Anyone who runs for governor must have three qualifications: He or she must be at least 25 years old, a citizen of the United States for five years before the election, and a resident of Louisiana for at least five years. The governor serves a four-year term that begins at noon on the second Monday in March following the election. The governor appoints people to other important offices, such as the attorney general and the secretary of state.

BOBBY JINDAL: LOUISIANA GOVERNOR

Bobby Jindal (1971–) is the son of immigrants from India. He grew up in Baton Rouge and changed his name from Piyush to Bobby when he was a child. After graduating from Brown University in Rhode Island, he studied health care systems at Oxford University in England. He returned to Louisiana where he was secretary of the Department of Health and Hospitals. In 2001, Jindal became the assistant secretary for the Department of Health and Human Services for President George W. Bush. He was elected governor of Louisiana in 2007. Jindal's book, *Leadership and Crisis*, tells about his experience helping Louisiana through the devastating *Deepwater Horizon* oil spill.

? Want to know more? Visit www.factsfornow .scholastic.com and enter the keyword **Louisiana**.

Representing Louisiana

This list shows the number of elected officials who represent Louisiana, both on the state and national levels:

OFFICE	NUMBER	LENGTH OF TERM
State senators	39	4 years
State representatives	105	4 years
U.S. senators	2	6 years
U.S. representatives	6	2 years
Presidential electors	8	—

The second in command in the executive branch is the lieutenant governor, who also is elected for a term of four years. The lieutenant governor heads the state senate, appoints senate committees, and oversees the work of other state departments.

THE LEGISLATIVE BRANCH

The state legislature, also called the general assembly, meets in the capitol in Baton Rouge. The assembly has two houses: the senate, which includes 39 members, and the house of representatives, with 105 members. Each senator and representative has to be at least 18 years old and a registered voter. He or she must have lived in Louisiana for two years before the election and in the district for at least one year. Everyone in the legislature is elected to four-year terms.

The biggest job for the legislators is to create and introduce new bills. Once a bill has been favorably voted on by a majority (more than half) of the legislators in both houses, it goes to the governor. The

The courtroom of the Louisiana Supreme Court is housed in a white granite and marble building, located on Royal Street in New Orleans's French Quarter.

governor has three choices: sign the bill into law, let it become a law without a signature, or veto the law. But a veto is not the last word! The legislature can vote on the bill again, and if two-thirds of both houses vote yes, the law passes.

THE JUDICIAL BRANCH

The highest court in the state is the supreme court. Seven judges make up this court: a chief justice and six associate justices. Their job is to interpret Louisiana laws to make sure they don't conflict with the state constitution or federal laws.

Judges who want to be on the supreme court have to meet a lot of special qualifications. They must be state citizens, they must be lawyers who have passed the Louisiana bar exam (a test for lawyers), and they must have practiced law for at least five years.

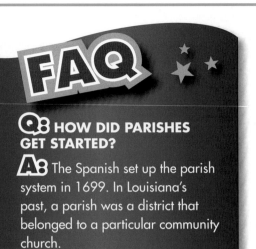

Q8 HOW DID PARISHES GET STARTED?

A8 The Spanish set up the parish system in 1699. In Louisiana's past, a parish was a district that belonged to a particular community church.

LOCAL GOVERNMENT

Louisiana doesn't have counties like other states. Instead, the state is divided into parishes. Today, Louisiana has 64 parish governments. Forty-one of them are run by a system called police juries (though they have nothing to do with the police). The rest

Louisiana Parishes

This map shows the 64 parishes in Louisiana. Baton Rouge, the state capital, is indicated with a star.

operate under a system of home rule. That means they govern themselves in local matters.

In parishes with police juries, the people elect any-where from 5 to 15 members to sit on the jury. In areas with home rule, voters elect commissioners to run their local government. Members of both police juries and commissioners serve four-year terms.

Poverty, race relations, education, and hurricane preparation and recovery are the main challenges that Louisiana's government faces every day. Following Hurricane Katrina, the city government of New Orleans faced enormous obstacles as it rebuilt the city. Other local governments also grapple with how to help all Louisianans have better, safer lives.

KIDS GET INVOLVED

Everyone in Louisiana has a voice in the government, and kids are no exception. In 2006, eighth-grader Joseph Louviere noticed that something was missing from the state flag! The flag included an image of a pelican feeding her chicks. Okay so far. But all tradi-tional images of a pelican and her nest include three drops of blood on the mother's breast. The blood sym-bolizes sacrifice. But the blood drops were not on the Louisiana flag.

Joseph contacted his state senator, Damon Baldone, and explained the problem. As a result, the House Judiciary Committee unanimously recommended House Bill 833, which requires all Louisiana state flags to show three drops of blood on the pelican's breast. To Joseph, and to the legislators who helped craft the bill, the new addition to the flag is especially appropri-ate because of the months and years of rebuilding and renewal following Hurricane Katrina.

State Flag

In 1812, Louisiana became the 18th state to join the Union. Its flag consisted of a star in a red square in the upper-left corner and 13 alternating red, white, and blue horizontal stripes. During the Civil War, Louisiana changed its flag in 1861 and again in 1863. In 1912, the Louisiana legislature adopted the present flag. It is a blue banner that features the state seal, which depicts a mother pelican in a nest with three young pelicans and the state motto, "Union, Justice and Confidence."

State Seal

Louisiana's first territorial governor, William C. C. Claiborne, admired the eastern brown pelican, a large waterbird that lived along the Gulf Coast. He was impressed with the fact that the bird fed its young with pieces of its own flesh when food was scarce. The governor depicted the pelican on all of his official correspondence.

This version was adopted on April 30, 1902, in the official state seal. In April 2006, the state legislature passed a bill requiring that the seal and flag include three drops of blood to show the mother pelican's sacrifice for her young.

The state motto, "Union, Justice and Confidence," are featured on the seal.

READ ABOUT

A fisher empties
his wire trap of
crawfish.

CHAPTER EIGHT

ECONOMY

★

LOUISIANA'S ECONOMY IS BASED ALMOST ENTIRELY ON OIL, NATURAL GAS, FORESTLAND, FISHING, AND AGRICULTURE. Tourism is big business in many areas of the state, especially New Orleans. Other industries, such as shipbuilding and aerospace, provide jobs and healthy income to the state's workers.

Workers prepare drilling machinery on an oil rig

WORD TO KNOW

offshore platform *a fixed structure where wells are drilled offshore*

OIL, GAS, AND CHEMICAL MANUFACTURING

Louisiana is a world leader in the oil and gas businesses: the state claims the first oil well in 1901 and the first **offshore platform** in the 1940s. Today, the oil and natural gas industries are the backbone of the state's economy. And they should be—Louisiana is one of the top oil-producing states and the number two gas-producing state in the country. Almost 10 percent of all known U.S. oil reserves lie in the ground beneath Louisiana!

Those numbers mean that Louisiana provides more than 25 percent of the nation's daily oil and natural gas production. Each year, the oil and gas industries bring billions of dollars into Louisiana. Oil companies employ about 17 percent of all Louisiana workers.

Major Agricultural and Mining Products

This map shows where Louisiana's major agricultural and mining products come from. See a cow? That means cattle are raised there!

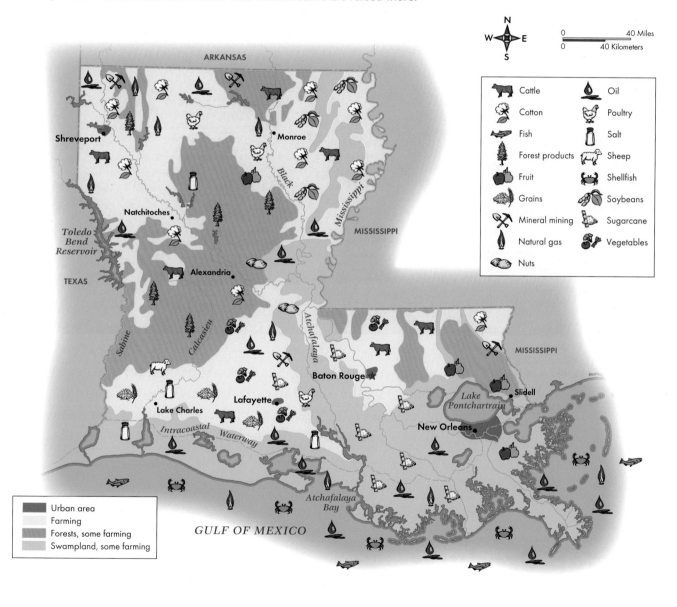

ARKANSAS

Shreveport

Monroe

Natchitoches

Toledo Bend Reservoir

TEXAS

Alexandria

MISSISSIPPI

Black

Mississippi

Sabine

Calcasieu

Atchafalaya

Baton Rouge

MISSISSIPPI

Lake Pontchartrain

Slidell

New Orleans

Lafayette

Lake Charles

Intracoastal Waterway

Atchafalaya Bay

GULF OF MEXICO

Legend:

Symbol	Product	Symbol	Product
Cattle		Oil	
Cotton		Poultry	
Fish		Salt	
Forest products		Sheep	
Fruit		Shellfish	
Grains		Soybeans	
Mineral mining		Sugarcane	
Natural gas		Vegetables	
Nuts			

- Urban area
- Farming
- Forests, some farming
- Swampland, some farming

Sugarcane is still a leading crop in Louisiana. Here a farmer sets fire to layers of cut sugarcane to burn off the stalks' outer layer.

In a single year, Louisiana's petroleum refineries make 15 billion gallons (57 billion liters) of gasoline. More than 100 chemical plants throughout the state make chemicals for businesses and industries, fertilizers, rubber, and all kinds of plastics.

Top Products

Agriculture Sugarcane, cotton, soybeans, forestry
Mining Oil, natural gas, salt, sulfur
Fishing Seafood, catfish

The ExxonMobil Refinery at Baton Rouge is the second-largest (in capacity) oil refinery on the North American continent.

AGRICULTURE, FORESTRY, AND FISHING

People with a sweet tooth can thank Louisiana for producing more than 12 million tons of sugarcane a year. Sugarcane is Louisiana's top crop, along with cotton, rice, soybeans, and corn. Millions of acres of Louisiana farmland is devoted to growing just those five crops, with other farms growing sweet potatoes, wheat, and hay. With its rich, fertile farmlands, it's no wonder that agriculture is big business in Louisiana.

Much of Louisiana's land is used for pastures and livestock. The warm, wet weather means grass grows all year long—which is ideal for raising cattle, hogs, and sheep.

Louisiana's forests bring in a lot of revenue for the state. Careful harvesting of the 13.9 million acres (5.6 million ha) of forests means about 1 billion **board feet** of wood is cut each year. All this wood is used to make paper, plywood, furniture, cardboard, and flooring.

Fishing is an important part of Louisiana's economy, too. About 25 percent of all the seafood caught in North America comes from Louisiana. This state produces more shrimp and oysters than any other.

EDMUND MCILHENNY: A HOT IDEA

At the end of the Civil War, banker Edmund McIlhenny (1815–1890) was broke. Friends and family persuaded him to plant something on his plantation on Avery Island, a salt-dome island off the Louisiana coast. He planted a crop of hot peppers from Mexico. When they were ripe, he used the peppers and the salt from the island to create a spicy sauce he called Tabasco (above). Then he bottled his concoction in cologne bottles and set off to sell them.

And sell they did! People loved the flavor of Tabasco, and pretty soon McIlhenny was selling Tabasco all over the United States. By the late 1870s, Tabasco had gone worldwide. Today, the Tabasco factory produces more than 3 million gallons (11 million L) of sauce a year. That's enough to fill more than four Olympic-size swimming pools!

? Want to know more? Visit www.factsfornow.scholastic.com and enter the keyword **Louisiana**.

WORD TO KNOW

board feet *units of lumber; a board foot is a piece of lumber that's 1 foot (30 centimeters) long, 1 foot wide, and 1 inch (2.5 cm) thick*

What Do Louisianans Do?

This color-coded chart shows what industries Louisianans work in.

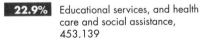

WOW

More than 1 billion pounds (454 million kg) of fish and shellfish come out of Louisiana's rivers, swamps, bayous, seacoasts, lakes, and streams every year!

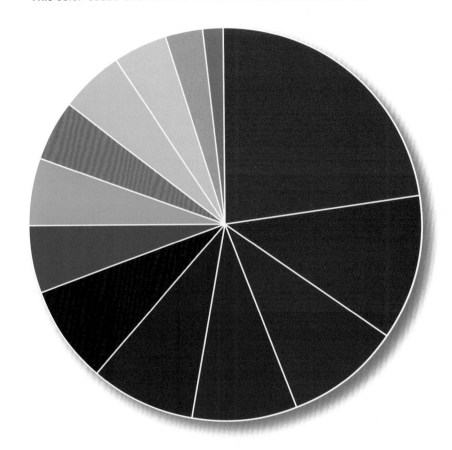

22.9% Educational services, and health care and social assistance, 453,139

11.9% Retail trade, 235,157

9.6% Arts, entertainment, and recreation, and accommodation and food services, 189,986

8.6% Construction, 170,534

8.4% Professional, scientific, and management, and administrative and waste management services, 164,919

8.2% Manufacturing, 162,869

5.6% Public administration, 110,629

5.4% Finance and insurance, and real estate and rental and leasing, 106,085

5.2% Transportation and warehousing, and utilities, 102,454

5.2% Other services, except public administration, 102,067

4.5% Agriculture, forestry, fishing and hunting, and mining, 88,508

2.9% Wholesale trade, 57,254

1.6% Information, 31,366

Source: U.S. Census Bureau, 2010 census

COMMERCE, SHIPBUILDING, AEROSPACE, AND CONSTRUCTION

The reason Thomas Jefferson wanted to purchase Louisiana was to get control of the Mississippi River. That would help the United States become a world player in international trade and business. Today, Louisiana is a big part of international business, both importing and exporting. Its five major ports handle about 450 million tons of cargo every year.

When Hurricane Katrina devastated the Louisiana coast, it damaged not only the ports, but also the roads, waterways, and railroads that took goods and cargo to and from the ports in other parts of Louisiana. Ocean traffic was chaotic for months during the rebuilding.

With its important ports and ocean traffic, shipbuilding is a big business in Louisiana. A large portion of the ships made in the United States are built in Louisiana. The University of New Orleans has the top shipbuilding school in the nation.

One of the big goals of the National Aeronautics and Space Administration (NASA) is to take humans to the moon and Mars and out into deep space. That's where Louisiana comes into the picture. New Orleans

MINI-BIO

MADAM C. J. WALKER: SELF-MADE MILLIONAIRE

One of the brightest stars in the Louisiana economy of the late 19th century was Sarah Breedlove McWilliams Walker (1867–1919), better known as Madam C. J. Walker. She was born in rural Louisiana, the daughter of former slaves. During the 1890s, she suffered from a mysterious scalp ailment that caused her to lose some of her hair. She experimented with home remedies until she found something that cured her.

She changed her name to Madam C. J. Walker, named her product Madam Walker's Wonderful Hair Grower, and went into business. At her death, Madam Walker left behind a fortune and a successful corporation. She once said, "If I have accomplished anything in life it is because I have been willing to work hard."

 Want to know more? Visit www.factsfornow.scholastic.com and enter the keyword **Louisiana**.

Workers at the Michoud Assembly Facility in New Orleans prepare a fuel tank used for the space shuttle.

is the home of the National Center for Advanced Manufacturing, which is developing all kinds of technologies to build a new type of space vehicle. Another New Orleans manufacturer, Michoud, is busy developing new ideas and materials that will help NASA make cutting-edge space-transport systems.

Hurricanes Katrina and Isaac left behind miles of destruction. Hundreds of thousands of homes and apartments have to be repaired or rebuilt. The massive job of rebuilding has created huge opportunities for workers in the construction industry. Louisiana added nearly 12,000 jobs in the construction industry between mid-2012 and mid-2013, an increase of 9.4 percent. New Orleans is planning to spend more than $23.5 billion on construction from 2013 to 2018. These projects will include new or rebuilt hospitals, modernized transportation systems, public housing, and improvements to the city's vital levee system. The construction boom will benefit neighborhoods and create safer and more attractive places to live and work.

SERVICE INDUSTRIES

The fastest-growing part of Louisiana's economy is the gambling industry. Casinos in areas such as Shreveport, New Orleans, and Baton Rouge draw millions of visitors to the state every year. This brings millions of dollars into the economy. The state has welcomed this new industry and is working with casino owners to ensure that gambling establishments remain a part of Louisiana's economy.

Louisiana casinos have helped strengthen the state's economy.

Hotels, restaurants, stores, theaters, hospitals, banks, warehouses, museums, and schools are all a part of the service industry. They provide jobs and revenue for the state.

It's taking time, but businesses are coming back to southern Louisiana, creating new service jobs and opportunities. In New Orleans, many restaurants and hotels reopened, and others continued to rebound from the hurricane damage. In the areas not affected by the hurricanes, the service industry continued to thrive. As major transportation arteries such as docks, ships, railroads, and roads have been rebuilt, Louisiana's economy has largely regained its strength statewide.

ARKANSAS

Plain Dealing

Bastrop

N
W E
S

Bossier
City

Minden

Doyline   Ruston

Monroe

20

Shreveport

West
Monroe

Ouchita

Black

Mississippi

0   40 Miles
0   40 Kilometers

Natchitoches

Many

Red

Kisatchie
National
Forest

MISSISSIPPI

*Toledo
Bend
Reservoir*

49

Pineville

Alexandria

Geographic
Center of
Louisiana

TEXAS

Marksville

Bunkie

55

Bogalusa

De Ridder

Amite

Lake
Pontchartrain

Atchafalaya

Ville Platte

Washington
Opelousas

**Baton
Rouge**

Baker   Hammond

59   MISSISSIPPI

Sabine

Eunice

Grand Coteau

12

Shenandoah

10

Sulphur

Calcasieu

Lafayette

White
Castle

Carville

Slidell

10

Lake
Charles

Jennings

Crowley

St. Martinville

Darrow

10

Kenner
Metairie

**New
Orleans**

New Iberia

Abbeville

Donaldsonville

Intracoastal

Avery Island

Johnson's
Bayou

Waterway

Morgan
City

Thibodaux

Bayou
Cane

Houma

GULF OF MEXICO

10 — Interstate highway

ALABA

TRAVEL GUIDE

★

FROM THE QUIET NORTHERN FORESTS TO THE SMALL TOWNS OF CAJUN COUNTRY, FROM THE MYSTERIOUS SWAMPLANDS TO THE LIVELY ALLEYWAYS OF SHREVEPORT AND BATON ROUGE, LOUISIANA IS A STATE THAT BEARS A CLOSER LOOK. People who take time to explore the hidden Louisiana find a state filled with warmth, great food, friendly people, and exciting things to do and see.

← Follow along with this travel map. We'll begin in New Orleans and travel around, all the way to Monroe!

GREATER NEW ORLEANS

THINGS TO DO: Tour the historic French Quarter in New Orleans, sample Creole food, or enjoy the cultural excitement of Mardi Gras or the annual Jazz Festival!

New Orleans

★ **National World War II Museum:** Oral histories, powerful images, and extraordinary artifacts illustrate the courage, teamwork, and sacrifice of the men and women who served during World War II.

★ **The New Orleans Jazz National Historical Park:** This park celebrates a uniquely American genre of music. Enjoy a scenic walk to hear jazz ensembles and concerts.

★ **Fire Department Museum:** The Washington Avenue Firehouse is now the home of the New Orleans Fire Department Museum, an educational facility that features two floors of firefighting memorabilia.

★ **Old U.S. Mint:** Built in 1835, the Old U.S. Mint, where money is printed, is the only building in America to have served both as a U.S. and a Confederate mint.

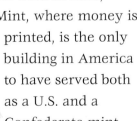

★ **Confederate Museum:** Memorial Hall Civil War Museum, also known as the Confederate Museum, is the oldest operating museum in Louisiana. Built by the Louisiana Historical Association in 1891, it houses war records, artifacts, and memorabilia of the Civil War.

★ **New Orleans Museum of Art:** The museum houses a $200 million collection in its 46 galleries, featuring French, Spanish, and American works of art.

★ **Tulane Museum of Natural History:** This museum holds an extensive collection of artifacts from the region's natural history, including the world's largest collection of post-larval fishes—more than 7 million specimens in more than 200,000 lots.

African artifacts at the New Orleans Museum of Art

Bourbon Street in New Orleans's French Quarter

★ **French Quarter:** Take a walk down historic Bourbon Street and take in all of the fun and excitement of the historic French Quarter. The architecture of the buildings is really unique.

The Causeway, the world's longest bridge over water, stretches for 24 miles (39 km) over Lake Pontchartrain.

PLANTATION COUNTRY

THINGS TO DO: Visit the state capitol in Baton Rouge, catch some football, or tour historic plantations.

Baton Rouge

★ **Louisiana State University:** Tour the campus and catch an LSU Tigers football game!

★ **LSU Museum of Natural Science:** The museum is divided into two main parts: the public exhibits containing both habitat and biological exhibits, along with identification panels; and the research collections used by scientists from all over the world.

★ **Louisiana State Capitol:** The country's tallest capitol at 34 stories high; come and walk through the halls of this state gem where important decisions regarding Louisiana are made every day.

★ **Capitol Park Museum:** Permanent exhibits highlight those aspects of the state's history that are nationally significant, as well as those aspects of the state's culture that are unique, including the Creole and Cajun cultures.

★ **BREC's Baton Rouge Zoo:** More than 1,800 animals await you in the beautifully landscaped zoo. See alligators, elephants, giraffes, flamingos, and white tigers.

Amite

★ **Blythewood Plantation:** This plantation, which is more than 100 years old, is filled with Victorian and heirloom antiques.

Darrow

★ **Houmas House Plantation and Gardens:** This home belonged to plantation owner John Burnside and was known as the Sugar Palace.

SEE IT HERE!

CHECK OUT MR. CHARLIE!

If oil is your thing, don't miss the International Petroleum Museum and Exposition in Morgan City. There you'll see Mr. Charlie, a huge, real oil rig! Mr. Charlie was in the oil-drilling business from 1954 to 1986, drilling hundreds of wells off the coast of Morgan City, Louisiana. He's a pretty standard oil rig. His barge (the foundation) is about 220 feet (67 m) long and 85 feet (26 m) wide. The crew of 58 lived on the rig full time. Mr. Charlie was retired in 1986 and is now part of the permanent display at the museum.

The grand staircase at Chretien Point Plantation in Sunset was reproduced for Tara, Scarlett O'Hara's home in the movie *Gone with the Wind.*

CAJUN COUNTRY

THINGS TO DO: Visit this breathtaking bayou region, enjoy authentic gumbo and real Cajun food, and listen to unique musical instruments.

Atchafalaya Swamp

Lafayette

★ **Atchafalaya Swamp:** Take a thrilling boat tour around this stunning natural attraction that features 38 species of birds, alligators, mink, deer, squirrels, and other wildlife.

★ **Lafayette Art Association and Gallery:** See art originals, prints, pottery, glass, photography, wood and metal sculptures, and jewelry from the region.

Acadian Village

★ **Louisiana Folk Roots:** This is a cultural preservation and nonprofit organization presenting year-round educational workshops on instrument instruction, culture and language, Louisiana nature, and cuisine.

★ **Odell Pottery Studio:** Award-winning pottery studio, where you can experience the timeless magic of the potter's wheel, see a spectacular raku firing, and enjoy a unique shopping experience with all-American handmade fine crafts.

★ **Acadian Village:** This is Lafayette's original museum of authentic Acadian homes; it features a blacksmith shop, a doctor's museum, and a quaint chapel.

★ **Alexandre Mouton House/ Lafayette Museum:** Visit this lovely house museum and collection of Acadian history and culture. The original structure was built in the early 1800s as a Sunday House by Vermillionville's founder, Jean Mouton. It became the home of Governor Alexandre Mouton.

Saint Martinville

★ **Evangeline Oak:** Take a picture or two in front of this beautiful oak tree, which served as an inspiration for Longfellow's poem. It is the most photographed tree in the world!

Avery Island

★ **Tabasco Pepper Sauce Factory:** Tour this factory to learn about the history of the product and the process of making the world-famous hot sauce.

Tabasco Pepper Sauce Factory

Eunice

★ **Liberty Theater:** This theater is the home of the *Rendezvous des Cajuns* radio and TV show, better known as the Cajun Grand Ole Opry.

SEE IT HERE!

VERMILLIONVILLE

Take a tour back in time to Vermillionville, a beautiful 23-acre (9-ha) Cajun/Creole heritage and folklife park that re-creates life in the Acadian area from 1765 to 1890. The costumed craftspeople, live music, and cooking demonstrations will give you an authentic taste of Acadian life.

A quilter at the Vermillionville Cajun/Creole folk village

CROSSROADS

THINGS TO DO: Go swimming in Kincaid Lake, hike the Wild Azalea National Recreation Trail, or visit any number of plantations located in this beautiful central part of the state!

Alexandria

★ **Kincaid Lake Recreation Area:** Enjoy fishing, swimming, and skiing in this crystal clear lake, which is part of the Kisatchie National Forest Preserve.

★ **Wild Azalea National Recreation Trail:** Hike through 31 miles (50 km) of beautiful forestland and countryside.

Pineville

★ **Kisatchie National Forest:** Enjoy miles and miles of hiking, fishing, skiing, swimming, and other outdoor activities that will inspire visitors to connect with the outdoors more often!

Many

★ **Toledo Bend Reservoir:** Enjoy this breathtaking 185,000-acre (75,000-ha) reservoir, which boasts some of the best fishing, hunting, canoeing, and birding in the country.

SPORTSMAN'S PARADISE

THINGS TO DO: Hike through thick, piney woods that flourish with wildlife, visit mysterious bayous, and check out clear, sparkling lakes filled with bass and trout.

Shreveport

★ **American Rose Center:** The center features winding paths, babbling brooks, and some of the grandest and rarest roses in the world.

★ **Ark-La-Tex Antique Museum and Classic Vehicle Museum:** This museum offers an impressive assembly of antique fire trucks, vintage motorcycles, Graham trucks, and Dodge cars, as well as the duds those dashing drivers wore on the road!

Monroe

★ **Biedenharn Museum & Gardens:** View the home of the first Coca-Cola bottler, a candy maker named Joseph Biedenharn.

★ **Ouachita River:** Enjoy boating and canoeing along the Ouachita River, one of the more beautiful and scenic rivers in the South.

SEE IT HERE!

SCI-PORT

One of the biggest and coolest science museums in the state, Sci-Port science center in Shreveport is filled with hands-on exhibits. You can pet an alligator, build your own skeleton, and watch as leaf-cutter ants scurry around their huge anthill home. And don't forget to check out the science movies on the museum's 60-foot (18 m) IMAX dome theater.

Watching a baby alligator at Sci-Port

WRITING PROJECTS

Check out these ideas for creating campaign brochures and writing you-are-there editorials. Or research the migration paths of settlers and explorers.

118

ART PROJECTS

Create a great PowerPoint presentation, illustrate the state song, or learn about the state quarter and design your own.

119

TIMELINE

122

What happened when? This timeline highlights important events in the state's history—and shows what was happening throughout the United States at the same time.

FAST FACTS

Use this section to find fascinating facts about state symbols, land area and population statistics, weather, sports teams, and much more.

126

GLOSSARY

125

Remember the Words to Know from the chapters in this book? They're all collected here.

SCIENCE, TECHNOLOGY, ENGINEERING, & MATH PROJECTS

120

Make weather maps, graph population statistics, and research endangered species that live in the state.

PRIMARY VS. SECONDARY SOURCES

121

So what are primary and secondary sources and what's the diff? This section explains all that and where you can find them.

BIOGRAPHICAL DICTIONARY

This at-a-glance guide highlights some of the state's most important and influential people. Visit this section and read about their contributions to the state, the country, and the world.

133

RESOURCES

Books and much more. Take a look at these additional sources for information about the state.

138

WRITING PROJECTS

Write a Memoir, Journal, or Editorial for Your School Newspaper!

Picture Yourself . . .

★ standing in a huge stadium. Thousands of fans are screaming just for you. Even your parents are in the stands, waving and cheering. You're a chunkey champion!

　SEE: Chapter Two, page 31.

★ as a young settler in colonial New Orleans. It's crowded, but you don't care. It's hot, but you hardly even notice. Everywhere you go in this new town of New Orleans, the excitement is so thick you can almost see it.

　SEE: Chapter Three, pages 40–41.

Create an Election Brochure or Web site!

Run for office!

Throughout this book, you've read about some of the issues that concern Louisiana today. As a candidate for governor of Louisiana, create a campaign brochure or Web site. Explain how you meet the qualifications to be governor of Louisiana, and talk about the three or four major issues you'll focus on if you're elected. Remember, you'll be responsible for Louisiana's budget. How would you spend the taxpayers' money?

SEE: Chapter Seven, pages 90–92.

Compare and Contrast—When, Why, and How Did They Come?

Compare the migration and explorations of the first Native people and the first Europeans. Tell about:

• When their migrations began

• How they traveled

• Why they migrated

• Where their journeys began and ended

• What they found when they arrived

SEE: Chapters Two and Three, pages 24–25 and 34–35.

ART PROJECTS

Create a PowerPoint Presentation or Visitors' Guide

Welcome to Louisiana!

Louisiana is a great place to visit and to live! From its natural beauty to its bustling cities and historic sites, there's plenty to see and do. In your PowerPoint presentation or brochure, highlight 10 to 15 of Louisiana's amazing landmarks. Be sure to include:

★ a map of the state showing where these sites are located

★ photos, illustrations, Web links, natural history facts, geographic stats, climate and weather, plants and wildlife, recent discoveries

SEE: Chapter Nine, pages 108–115.

Illustrate the Lyrics to the Louisiana State Song ("Give Me Louisiana")

Use markers, paints, photos, collage, colored pencils, or computer graphics to illustrate the lyrics to "Give Me Louisiana," the state song. Turn your illustrations into a picture book, or scan them into a PowerPoint and add music.

SEE: The lyrics to "Give Me Louisiana" on page 128.

Research Louisiana's State Quarter

From 1999 to 2008, the U.S. Mint introduced new quarters commemorating each of the 50 states in the order that they were admitted into the Union. Each state's quarter features a unique design on its reverse, or back.

★ Go to www.factsfornow.scholastic.com. Enter the keyword **Louisiana** and look for the link to the Louisiana quarter.

★ Research the significance of each image. Who designed the quarter? Who chose the final design?

★ Design your own Louisiana quarter. What images would you choose for the reverse?

★ Make a poster showing the Louisiana quarter and label each image.

SCIENCE, TECHNOLOGY, ENGINEERING, & MATH PROJECTS

Graph Population Trends!

★ Compare population statistics (such as ethnic background, birth, death, and literacy rates) in Louisiana parishes or major cities.

★ In your graph or chart, look at population density, and write sentences describing what the population statistics show; graph one set of population statistics, write a paragraph explaining what the graphs reveal.

SEE: Chapter Six, pages 70–75 and 82–83.

Create a Weather Map of Louisiana!

Use your knowledge of Louisiana's geography to research and identify conditions that result in specific weather events, including thunderstorms and hurricanes. What is it about the geography of Louisiana that makes it vulnerable to things such as hurricanes? Create a weather map or poster that shows the weather patterns over the state. To accompany your map, explain the technology used to measure weather phenomena such as hurricanes, and provide data.

SEE: Chapter One, pages 14–16.

Black bear

Track Endangered Species

Using your knowledge of Louisiana's wildlife, research what animals and plants are endangered or threatened. Find out what the state is doing to protect these species. Chart known populations of the animals and plants, and report on changes in certain geographical areas

SEE: Chapter One, page 22.

PRIMARY VS. SECONDARY SOURCES

What's the Diff?

Your teacher may require at least one or two primary sources and one or two secondary sources for your assignment. So, what's the difference between the two?

★ **Primary sources are original.** You are reading the actual words of someone's diary, journal, letter, autobiography or interview. Primary sources can also be photographs, maps, prints, cartoons, news/film footage, posters, first-person newspaper articles, drawings, musical scores, and recordings. By the way, when you conduct a survey, interview someone, shoot a video, or take photographs to include in a project, are creating primary sources!

★ **Secondary sources are what you find in encyclopedias, textbooks, articles, biographies, and almanacs.** These are written by a person or group of people who tell about something that happened to someone else. Secondary sources also recount what another person said or did. This book is an example of a secondary source.

Now that you know what primary sources are—where can you find them?

★ **Your school or local library:** Check the library catalog for collections of original writings, government documents, musical scores, and so on. Some of this material may be stored on microfilm.

★ **Historical societies:** These organizations keep historical documents, photographs, and other materials. Staff members can help you find what you are looking for. History museums are also great places to see primary sources firsthand.

★ **The Internet:** There are lots of sites that have primary sources you can download and use in a project or assignment.

Louisiana Purchase treaty

TIMELINE

★ ★ ★

Alvar Nuñez
Cabeza de Vaca

U.S. Events `1500` Louisiana Events

1519
Alonso Álvarez de Pineda maps the Gulf Coast.

1528
Alvar Nuñez Cabeza de Vaca
wanders through Louisiana.

1565
Spanish admiral Pedro Menéndez de
Avilés founds St. Augustine, Florida, the
oldest continuously occupied European
settlement in the continental United States.

1541
Hernando de Soto is the first European
to see the Mississippi River.

`1600`

1682
René-Robert Cavelier, Sieur de La Salle,
claims more than 1 million square miles (2.6
million sq km) of territory in the Mississippi
River basin for France, naming it Louisiana.

1682
René-Robert Cavelier, Sieur de La
Salle, names Louisiana.

1699
Pierre Le Moyne, Sieur d'Iberville, founds Fort
Maurepas, the first settlement in Louisiana.

`1700`

1718
Jean-Baptiste Le Moyne, Sieur de
Bienville, founds New Orleans.

Jean-Baptiste Le Moyne

1719
Scotsman John Law is given control of Louisiana;
enslaved Africans arrive in large numbers.

1722
A hurricane destroys most of New Orleans.

1745
Ursuline Convent in New Orleans is built.

U.S. Events

1776

Thirteen American colonies declare their independence from Great Britain, marking the beginning of the Revolutionary War.

Louisiana territory map

1812-15

The United States and Britain fight the War of 1812.

1830

The Indian Removal Act forces eastern Native American groups to relocate west of the Mississippi River.

1861-65

The American Civil War is fought between the Northern Union and the Southern Confederacy; it ends with the surrender of the Confederate Army, led by General Robert E. Lee.

1886

Apache leader Geronimo surrenders to the U.S. Army, ending the last major Native American rebellion against the expansion of the United States into the West.

Louisiana Events

1763

Spain wins control of Louisiana.

1794

Eli Whitney invents the cotton gin.

1800

1800

Napoleon convinces Spain to return control of Louisiana to France.

1803

Napoleon sells the Louisiana territory to the United States for $15 million.

1812

Louisiana becomes the 18th state; the War of 1812 begins.

1815

Andrew Jackson's forces win the Battle of New Orleans.

1838

The first Mardi Gras in New Orleans is held.

1843

Norbert Rillieux invents the sugar processing evaporator, greatly improving sugar production.

1861

Louisiana secedes from the Union.

1868

Louisiana's Reconstruction constitution is adopted.

1879

Baton Rouge becomes Louisiana's state capital.

1898

The new state constitution rolls back many of the rights held by African Americans.

U.S. Events `1900` Louisiana Events

1901
First oil field in the state is discovered near Jennings, Louisiana.

1909
Sulfur mining begins near Sulfur, Louisiana.

1916
Natural gas is discovered near Monroe, Louisiana.

1917-18
The United States engages in World War I.

1928
Huey P. Long becomes governor.

Huey P. Long

1929
The stock market crashes, plunging the United States more deeply into the Great Depression.

1941-45
The United States engages in World War II.

1960
Public schools in New Orleans are desegregated.

1964-73
The United States engages in the Vietnam War.

1977
Ernest "Dutch" Morial is elected the first black mayor of New Orleans.

1986
Oil prices drop to less than $10 a barrel.

1991
The United States and other nations fight the brief Persian Gulf War against Iraq.

1995
Shell Oil installs the Mars platform, the deepest oil platform in the world.

`2000`

2001
Terrorists hijack four U.S. aircraft and crash them into the World Trade Center in New York City, the Pentagon in Washington, D.C., and a Pennsylvania field, killing thousands.

2003
The United States and coalition forces invade Iraq.

2005
Hurricanes Katrina and Rita hit southern Louisiana.

2010
The *Deepwater Horizon* oil spill damages Louisiana's coastline.

GLOSSARY

alluvial plain an area that is created when sand, soil, and rocks are carried by water and dropped in a certain place

bisque a rich, creamy soup

board feet units of lumber; a board foot is a piece of lumber that's 1 foot (30 cm) long, 1 foot wide, and 1 inch (2.5 cm) thick

civil rights basic rights that are guaranteed to all citizens

colonized created colonies, which are settlements that are controlled by another government

confederacies groups allied together for a common cause

delta an alluvial deposit at the mouth of a river

discrimination the unfair treatment of a group, based on its race, age, gender, or other characteristic

étouffée a spicy, Cajun-style stew served over rice

exposure a condition of not being protected from severe weather

famine drastic loss of food, causing starvation and death

hardwood a tree that sheds its leaves at the end of the growing season

Jim Crow laws laws that were passed to enforce racial segregation and to prevent African Americans from doing things that white people could do

levees wall-like embankments, often made of earth, built along a river to control flooding

natural gas a gas that is formed in the earth when organic material decomposes under pressure

offshore platform a fixed structure where oil wells are drilled offshore

radiocarbon dating a process that dates an object by counting its radioactive decay of carbon

Reconstruction the period after the Civil War when the Southern states were reorganized and reestablished in the Union

seceded withdrew from a group

sediment material that is carried by water, wind, or glaciers

segregated the forced separation of one group from the rest of society

sharecroppers farmers who give a portion of their crops as rent for the land

subsidence the state of eroded areas sinking underwater

surges waves pushed onto land by the wind

FAST FACTS

★ ★ ★

State Symbols

Statehood date	April 30, 1812, the 18th state
Origin of state name	Named by Sieur de La Salle for the French king Louis XIV
State capital	Baton Rouge
State nickname	Pelican State
State motto	"Union, Justice and Confidence"
State bird	Eastern brown pelican
State flower	Magnolia bloom
State songs	"Give Me Louisiana" (see lyrics on page 128) and "You Are My Sunshine"
State tree	Bald cypress
State fair	Shreveport (October)

State seal

Geography

Total area; rank	51,840 square miles (134,265 sq km); 31st
Land; rank	43,562 square miles (112,825 sq km); 33rd
Water; rank	8,278 square miles (21,440 sq km); 5th
Inland water; rank	4,154 square miles (10,759 sq km); 5th
Coastal water; rank	1,935 square miles (5,012 sq km); 3rd
Territorial water; rank	2,189 square miles (5,669 sq km); 5th
Geographic center	Avoyelles, 3 miles (5 km) southeast of Marksville
Latitude	28° 00' N to 33° 00' N
Longitude	89° 00' W to 94° 00' W
Highest point	Driskill Mountain, 535 feet (163 km)
Lowest point	−8 feet (−2.4 m) at New Orleans
Largest city	New Orleans
Number of counties	64 parishes
Longest river	Mississippi River, 305 miles (491 km) in Louisiana of a total length of 2,348 miles (3,779 km)

State flag

Population

Population; rank (2010 census):	4,287,768; 25th
Density (2010 census):	98 persons per square mile (38 per sq km)
Population distribution (2010 census):	73% urban, 27% rural
Race (2010 census):	White persons: 60.3%
	Black persons: 31.8%
	Asian persons: 1.5%
	American Indian and Alaska Native persons: 0.6%
	People of two or more races: 1.3%
	Hispanic or Latino persons: 4.2%
	People of some other race: 0.1%

Weather

Record high temperature	114°F (46°C) at Plain Dealing on August 10, 1936
Record low temperature	−16°F (−27°C) at Minden on February 13, 1899
Average July temperature, New Orleans	83°F (28°C)
Average January temperature, New Orleans	53°F (12°C)
Average yearly precipitation, New Orleans	62 inches (157 cm)
Average July temperature, Shreveport	83°F (28°C)
Average January temperature, Shreveport	47°F (8°C)
Average yearly precipitation, Shreveport	69 inches (175 cm)

Mardi Gras

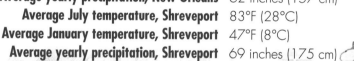

LOUISIANA'S STATE SONG

★ ★ ★

"Give Me Louisiana"

Words by Doralice Fontane
Music by Dr. John Croom

Louisiana has four state songs that were adopted beginning in 1952. The state has two official state songs, one official state environmental song, and one official state march song. The first official state song was Doralice Fontane's "Give Me Louisiana," which was incorporated by Legislative Act 431 of 1970 (excerpted below). The other official state song, "You Are My Sunshine," was written by former governor Jimmie H. Davis and Charles Mitchell and incorporated by Legislative Act 540 of 1977.

Give me Louisiana,
The State where I was born
The State of snowy cotton,
The best I've ever known;
A State of sweet magnolias,
And Creole melodies.

Oh give me Louisiana,
The State where I was born
Oh what sweet old mem'ries
The mossy old oaks bring.
It brings us the story
of our Evangeline.

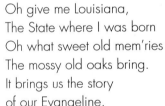

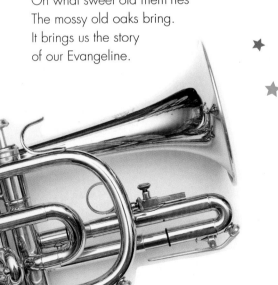

NATURAL AREAS

National Monument

Poverty Point National Monument commemorates a culture that thrived during the first and second millennia BCE. This site contains some of the largest prehistoric human-made earth formations in North America, covering more than 400 acres (162 ha) of land.

National Historical Park

Louisiana is home to three national historical parks, featuring the history and culture of the Bayou state, including the *Jean Lafitte National Historical Park and Preserve*, which protects significant examples of the rich natural and cultural resources of Louisiana's Mississippi River Delta region; the *Cane River Creole National Historical Park*, which preserves and protects various French and Creole architectural sites along the Cane River; and the *New Orleans Jazz National Historical Park*, which serves the great New Orleans community by showcasing the rich jazz heritage of the Bayou state.

National Forest

Kisatchie National Forest is Louisiana's sole national forest, covering about 604,000 acres (244,430 ha) in north-central Louisiana.

State Parks and Forests

The Louisiana state park system consists of more than 35 state parks, preservation areas, and commemorative areas, including *Bayou Segnette State Park, Chicot State Park, Tickfaw State Park*, and *Cypremort Point State Park*. The *Louisiana State Arboretum* is the nation's oldest state-supported arboretum, containing more than 150 species of plant life native to the region. *Alexander State Forest*, located in central Louisiana, is the only state forest.

SPORTS TEAMS

★ ★ ★

NCAA Teams (Division I)

Grambling State University *Tigers*
Louisiana State University *Fighting Tigers*
Louisiana Tech University *Bulldogs*
McNeese State University *Cowboys*
Nicholls State University *Colonels*
Northwestern State University *Demons*
Southeastern Louisiana University *Lions*
Southern University–Baton Rouge *Jaguars*
Tulane University *Green Wave*
University of New Orleans *Privateers*
University of Louisiana–Lafayette *Ragin' Cajuns*
University of Louisiana–Monroe *Warhawks*

PROFESSIONAL SPORTS TEAMS

★ ★ ★

National Basketball Association
New Orleans *Pelicans*

National Football League
New Orleans *Saints*

CULTURAL INSTITUTIONS

Libraries

State Library of Louisiana (Baton Rouge) provides information and support to the state's parish libraries.

Museums

Louisiana State Museum (New Orleans, Baton Rouge, and other locations), *Louisiana Historical Society* (New Orleans), and *Louisiana State Exhibit Museum* (Shreveport) all house fine collections on state and regional history.

Jean Lafitte National Historical Park and Preserve (New Orleans) includes an area where part of the Battle of New Orleans was fought during the War of 1812. The park also includes the *Cajun Cultural Center* and a service that offers tours of the French Quarter of New Orleans.

Performing Arts

The *Louisiana Philharmonic Orchestra* (New Orleans) is the region's only full-time professional orchestra. It offers more than 120 performances each year.

The *New Orleans Opera* (New Orleans) continues New Orleans' rich opera history with a wide variety of performances and educational activities.

Universities and Colleges

In 2011, Louisiana had 17 public and 15 private institutions of higher learning.

ANNUAL EVENTS

January–March

Sugar Bowl football game in New Orleans (January)

Mardi Gras in New Orleans and many other cities (Shrove Tuesday)

Audubon Pilgrimage in Saint Francisville (March)

Louisiana Black Heritage Festival in New Orleans (March)

April–June

Festival International de Louisiane in Lafayette (April)

Holiday in Dixie in Shreveport (April)

Ponchatoula Strawberry Festival in Ponchatoula (April)

Jazz and Heritage Festival in New Orleans (April–May)

Contraband Days in Lake Charles (May)

Tomato Festival in Chalmette (May)

Bayou Lacombe Crab Festival in Lacombe (June)

Louisiana Peach Festival in Ruston (June)

July–September

Tarpon Rodeo in Grand Isle (July)

Frog Festival in Rayne (August–November)

Bayou Lafourche Antiques Show and Sale in Thibodaux (September)

Best of the Bayou Food Festival in Houma (September)

Louisiana Shrimp and Petroleum Festival in Morgan City (September)

October–December

Bridge City Gumbo Festival in Bridge City (October)

Festivals Acadiens in Lafayette (October)

French Food Festival in Larose (October)

International Rice Festival in Crowley (October)

Louisiana State Fair in Shreveport (October–November)

Gueydan Duck Festival in Gueydan (November)

Hodges Garden Fall Art Festival in Many (November)

Natchitoches Christmas Festival of Lights in Natchitoches (November–December)

Bonfires on the Mississippi River Levee (Christmas Eve)

BIOGRAPHICAL DICTIONARY

Louis Armstrong

Reverend Avery Alexander (1910–1999) was a prominent Louisiana civil rights leader and legislator.

Louis Armstrong See page 78.

Evelyn Ashford (1957–), born in Shreveport, is a track-and-field runner who won four gold medals and one silver medal in three different Olympic Games. At one time, she was the women's world record holder in the 100-meter dash.

John James Audubon See page 21.

Israel Augustine (1924–1994), born in New Orleans, was the first African American district judge in Louisiana.

Daniel "Danny" Barker (1909–1994), born in New Orleans, was a famous New Orleans jazz musician.

P. G. T. Beauregard (1818–1893), born in St. Bernard Parish, was a Confederate general in the American Civil War. He led his troops to victory in the war's earliest fighting, the First Battle of Bull Run, in Virginia.

Geoffrey Beene (1927–2004), born in Haynesville, was a fashion designer who became famous for his unconventional designs in the 1960s. April 27 is "Geoffrey Beene Day" in Louisiana.

E. J. Bellocq (1873–1949), born in New Orleans, was a photographer who is remembered for his haunting photos of women in New Orleans. These have inspired novels, poems, and films.

Willie Birch (1942–) is an African American artist famous for his large black-and-white paintings that depict the culture of New Orleans.

Kathleen Babineaux Blanco (1942–), born in New Iberia, grew up in a family of farmers and small-business owners. She became the first woman from Lafayette Parish to be elected to the state legislature. She later served as public service commissioner and lieutenant governor. In January 2004, she became the first female governor of Louisiana.

Kathleen Blanco

Lindy Boggs (1916–2013) served as a member of the House of Representatives and later as a U.S. ambassador. She was the first woman from Louisiana to be elected to Congress.

Arna W. Bontemps (1902–1973), born in Alexandria, was an African American poet and writer. His famous children's book, *Story of the Negro*, received many literary awards.

Terry Bradshaw (1948–), born in Shreveport, is a Hall of Fame football player and former quarterback for the Pittsburgh Steelers.

Ruby Bridges See page 63.

Truman Capote (1924–1984), born in New Orleans, was a novelist famous for works including *In Cold Blood* and *Breakfast at Tiffany's*.

James Carville See page 90.

Kate Chopin (1850–1904) was an American author of short stories and novels. She was from Saint Louis, Missouri, but her writing was mostly about the Louisiana Creole culture. She is now considered to have been a forerunner of feminist authors of the 20th century.

Joseph Samuel Clark (1871–1944) was an educator and president of Southern University in Baton Rouge.

Harvey Lavan "Van" Cliburn (1934–2013), born in Shreveport, was a pianist who gained fame in his early twenties. He played for kings and queens, important politicians, and every U.S. president from Harry S. Truman (in office from 1945 to 1953) to Barack Obama.

Harry Connick Jr. (1967–) is a singer, pianist, actor, and humanitarian. His father was the district attorney of New Orleans, and his mother was a Louisiana supreme court justice. He was born in New Orleans.

Melissa Darden See page 32.

Harry Connick Jr.

Reverend Abraham Lincoln Davis (1914–1978) was a founder of the Southern Christian Leadership Conference. He was born in Terrebonne Parish.

Michael DeBakey (1908–2008), born in Lake Charles, was a world-class heart surgeon, known for his pioneering work in the field of heart surgery. He invented or perfected dozens of medical devices and procedures that have saved thousands of lives around the world. He was born in Lake Charles and got his medical degree from Tulane University in New Orleans.

Thomas C. Dent (1932–1998), born in New Orleans, was a famous writer, poet, and civil rights activist.

Fats Domino (1928–) is a famed musician who helped popularize rock and roll in the 1950s with stride and boogie-woogie influences in his piano playing. He was born in New Orleans.

Fats Domino

Caroline Dormon See page 18.

Mary Alice Fontenot (1910–2003), born in Eunice, wrote the Clovis Crawfish series of children's books, which featured animals from the Louisiana bayou. The books are sprinkled with Cajun words and explanations of their pronunciations and meanings.

Rivers Frederick (1874–1954) was a surgeon and founder of the United Negro College Fund. He was from New Roads and graduated from the University of New Orleans.

Ernest James Gaines (1933–) is an African American author, who was born in Pointe Coupee Parish in Baton Rouge. His works have been translated into many languages, including French, Spanish, German, Russian, and Chinese. *A Lesson Before Dying* and *The Autobiography of Miss Jane Pittman* are two of his best-known books. Four of his works have been made into movies.

Bernardo Gálvez See page 42.

Bernardo Gálvez

Shirley Ann Grau (1929–), born in New Orleans, is an author who won the Pulitzer Prize for her 1965 novel, *The Keepers of the House*.

Ron Guidry (1950–), born in Lafayette, is an award-winning baseball player and former All-Star pitcher for the New York Yankees.

Ernest Guiraud (1837–1892), born in New Orleans, was a famous French composer.

Bryant Gumbel (1948–) is a famous newscaster who now hosts the HBO show *Real Sports with Bryant Gumbel*. He was born in New Orleans.

Margaret Gaffney Haughery (1814?–1882) moved with her husband and their baby girl to New Orleans. Haughery opened a bakery and gave wagonloads of fresh bread and milk to the hungry. It became one of the best-known businesses in New Orleans.

Lillian Hellman (1905–1984), born in New Orleans, was a playwright who earned fame for *The Children's Hour* and *Little Foxes* in the 1930s.

George Joseph Herriman (1880–1944) was a cartoonist best known for writing and drawing the comic strip *Krazy Kat*, one of the most popular cartoons ever published. He was born in New Orleans.

Al Hirt (1922–1999) was a popular U.S. trumpeter and bandleader. He was born in New Orleans.

Clementine Hunter (1887–1988), born on Hidden Hill Plantation, was a folk artist known for her paintings that depicted plantation life during the mid-1800s.

Mahalia Jackson (1912–1972) was a gospel singer who became famous with the song "Move On Up a Little." She was the first to have a million-selling gospel record and is considered to be the best gospel singer in the history of the genre. She was born in New Orleans.

Mahalia Jackson

Jean Lafitte (1780?–1826?) was a famous pirate who worked for the Caribbean government. His life is legend in Louisiana.

Emeril Lagasse (1959–) is well-known to TV viewers. His popular cooking shows draw huge audiences who enjoy the spicy style of cooking he made famous as a New Orleans chef at his own Emeril's restaurant.

Pierre Le Moyne, Sieur d'Iberville See page 40.

Jerry Lee Lewis (1935–), born in Ferriday, is a singer who was one of the early pioneers of rock and roll. His famous songs include "Whole Lotta Shakin' Goin' On" and "Great Balls of Fire."

Archie Manning (1949–) was a former NFL quarterback for the New Orleans Saints between 1971 and 1982.

Eli Manning (1981–), born in New Orleans, is the NFL quarterback for the New York Giants.

Peyton Manning (1976–), born in New Orleans, is the quarterback for the Indianapolis Colts and has shattered NFL passing records since his arrival in the NFL. His career hit a high note on February 4, 2007, when the Colts defeated the Chicago Bears in Super Bowl XLI and Manning was named Super Bowl MVP.

Ellis Marsalis (1934–) is considered one of the premier pianists of modern jazz. His sons Branford, Wynton, Delfeayo, and Jason are also jazz musicians.

Edmund McIlhenny See page 103.

John Willis Menard See page 56.

Ernest Nathan "Dutch" Morial (1929–1989) was from a Creole family and grew up proud of his Louisiana heritage. In 1954, he became the first African American to receive a law degree from Louisiana State University in Baton Rouge. In 1977, he became the first African American mayor of New Orleans.

Melvin Thomas "Mel" Ott (1909–1958), born in Gretna, was a Hall of Fame baseball player who was a perennial All-Star for the New York Giants.

P. B. S. Pinchback (1837–1921), born a free black, was elected to the state senate in 1868 and became the state's governor in 1872. He was the first African American governor in the United States.

Archie (left), Eli (center), and Peyton (right) Manning

Alonso Álvarez de Pineda (1494–1519) was a Spanish explorer who mapped the Gulf of Mexico.

Paul Prudhomme (1940–) is a New Orleans chef who has made Cajun cooking famous. He's written cookbooks and cooked for royalty and heads of state around the world.

Henry Hobson Richardson (1838–1886), born in Saint James Parish, was a world-famous architect whose work left a significant influence in Chicago and Boston.

Cokie Roberts

Cokie Roberts (1943–) is a journalist and the senior news analyst for NPR. She was born in New Orleans.

Coleen Salley See page 80.

Kordell Stewart (1972–), born in Marrero, was an NFL football player known for a Hail Mary pass he threw in 1994, while in college. In the play known as the Miracle in Michigan, his team, the University of Colorado, defeated the University of Michigan 27–26.

Dorothy Mae Delavallade Taylor (1928–2000) was a New Orleans politician and the first African American woman elected to the Louisiana house of representatives.

Marie Therese (1742?–1817?), known as Coincoin (pronounced ko-kwi), was born into slavery. But by the time she died at around age 75, her descendants had become some of the wealthiest free blacks in the United States and founded the Cane River Creole community in Louisiana.

Alexander Pierre Tureaud Sr. (1899–1972) was a famous civil rights leader in Louisiana.

Madam C. J. Walker See page 105.

Edward Douglass White Jr. (1845–1921), born in Thibodeauxville, was a U.S. senator and the ninth chief justice of the United States. As a justice, he served as the head of the U.S. federal court system.

Fannie C. Williams (1882–1980) was a famous New Orleans educator who was instrumental in having a kindergarten class established for African Americans in the public school system.

T. Harry Williams (1909–1979) was an award-winning author and LSU professor known for his historical works.

Kordell Stewart

RESOURCES

★ ★ ★

BOOKS

Nonfiction

Benoit, Peter. *The BP Oil Spill.* New York: Children's Press, 2011.

Childress, Diana. *Barefoot Conquistador: Cabeza de Vaca and the Struggle for Native American Rights.* Minneapolis, Minn.: Twenty-First Century Books, 2008.

Frisch, Aaron. *New Orleans Saints.* Mankato, Minn.: Creative Education, 2014.

Henningfeld, Diane Andrews. *Hurricane Katrina.* Detroit: Greenhaven Press, 2010.

Hollar, Sherman. *Andrew Jackson.* New York: Britannica Educational Publishing, 2013.

McNeese, Tim. *The Louisiana Purchase: Growth of a Nation.* New York: Chelsea House, 2009.

Young, Jeff C. *Hernando de Soto: Spanish Conquistador in the Americas.* Berkeley Heights, N.J.: Enslow Publishers, 2009.

Fiction

Jameson, W. C. *Buried Treasures of the South: Legends of Lost, Buried, and Forgotten Treasures from Tidewater Virginia and Coastal Carolina to Cajun Louisiana.* Atlanta: August House Publishers, 2006.

Moore, Elizabeth, and Alice Couvillon. *Louisiana Indian Tales.* Gretna, La.: Pelican Publishing Company, 1990.

Reneaux, J. J. *Cajun Folktales.* Atlanta: August House Publishers, 1993.

Tallant, Robert. *Evangeline and the Acadians.* Gretna, La.: Pelican Publishing Company, 1996.

Willis Holt, Kimberly. *Part of Me: Stories of a Louisiana Family.* New York: Henry Holt, 2006.

Visit this Scholastic Web site for more information on Louisiana:
www.factsfornow.scholastic.com
Enter the keyword **Louisiana**

INDEX

★ ★ ★

AUTHOR'S TIPS AND SOURCE NOTES

★ ★ ★

Louisiana is one of those states that everyone knows a little about, so finding information was easy—at first. The books I consulted included the *Louisiana Almanac, It's My State! Louisiana* by Ruth Bjorklund, and the *Pelican Guide to Plantation Homes of Louisiana.*

In addition to using books and other written sources, I used Louisiana government and official Web sites, and sites for organizations with up-to-the-minute information, statistics, and resources. All of that information was still hard to verify, since everyone seemed to have different "facts" about the state, especially since Hurricane Katrina. My editors and I updated statistics as much as possible before this book went to press. In the end, finding source materials and information for this book was a combination of traditional research, careful Internet research from reliable sources, and lots of phone calls.

Photographs ©: age fotostock/John Cancalosi: 8; Animals Animals/C.C. Lockwood: 12, 20 top; AP Images: 90 top (Alex Brandon), 18 left (Alexandria Town Talk), 79 bottom (Burt Steel), 80 bottom (Chris Pizzello), 66 (Dave Martin), 127 (David Quinn), 136 (Ed Bailey), 115 (Jim Hudelson/The Shreveport Times), 93 (Judi Bottoni), 16, 59 bottom (NOAA), 79 top (Rex Features); Art Resource, NY: 34 top, 35 left (Jean-Gilles Berizzi/Reunion des Musees Nationaux), 43 (Culver Pictures); Bill Morris Literacy Foundation/Courtesy of Coleen Salley: 80 top; Clipart.com/ JupiterImages: 32; Corbis Images: 5 center right, 5 center left, 21, 25 top, 30, 39, 44 top, 45 left, 54, 58 bottom left, 60, 63, 121, 123 left, 124 (Bettmann), 69 (Brooks Kraft), 9 top, 20 bottom (Dan Guravich), 45 bottom (Danny Lehman), 114 (Dave G. Houser), 18 right,12 (David Muench), 106 (epa), 57 (J.C. Peters), 62 (John Vachon), 134 left (Justin Lane/epa), 83 (Lake County Museum), 119 left (Larry Lee Photography), 4 bottom, 137 left (Lynn Goldsmith), 113 top left (Mark E. Gibson), 68 (Michael Ainsworth/Dallas Morning News), 76 (Owen Franken), 113 bottom (Owen Franken), 14, 102 (Philip Gould); 137 right (Reuters), 58 bottom right, 64, 110 right (Robert Holmes); 61 (Russell Lee), 133 bottom (Shawn Thew/epa), 59 top, 65 (Steven Vidler/Eurasia Press), 24 bottom, 58 top, 59 left; Dreamstime/Michael Flippo: cover bottom; Getty Images: 70, 81, 127 (Cheryl Gerber), 111 (Chris Graythen), 78 bottom (Douglas Mason), 23 (Eastcott/Momatiuk), 135 right (GAB Archive), 84 (Harry How), 86 (Jim Schwabel), 105 (Michael Ochs Archives), 33 (MPI), 90 inset (Spencer Platt), 85 (Stuart Hannagan); iStockphoto: 116 top left, 117, 44 bottom right, 132 (Dave Huss/Graphically Speaking), 130 right (David Freund), 116 bottom, 130 left (Geoffrey Black), 5 top, 44 bottom center, 123 right (Hannamaria Photography), 110 left (Skip O'Donnell/Wish Photograf), 128 (Vladislav Lebedinski); JupiterImages: 77 right (Jan Oswald/Foodpix), 5 bottom right, 77 left (Paul Poplis/ FoodPix); Landov/David Grunfeld/The Times-Picayune: 90 top, 92; Louisiana Department of Culture, Recreation, and Tourism: 24 top, 25 left, 97, 126 top; Louisiana Secretary of State: 87 top, 96, 126 bottom; Nativestock.com/Marilyn "Angel" Wynn: 4 top center, 25 bottom, 27; NewOrleansOnline. com/Ron Calamia/GNOTCC: 73; North Wind Picture Archives: 51; Peter Arnold Inc./Jim Wark: 11; Redux/Imke Lass: cover inset; Retna Ltd./Leon Morris/Redferns: 134 right; Science Source/ John Eastcott & Yva Momatiuk: 98; ShutterStock, Inc./Mikko Pitkanen: 107; Smithsonian Institution, Washington, DC/D.E. Hurlbert: 31, 118 (D.E. Hurlbert); StockFood, Inc./TH Foto: 5 bottom left, 103, 113 top right (TH Foto); Superstock, Inc.: 99 top, 100 (Karl Kummels), cover (Photononstop), 88 (Steve Vidler); The Granger Collection, New York: 4 top right, 34 bottom, 35 top, 35 bottom, 36, 40 top, 40 bottom, 42, 45 top, 50, 52, 56, 122 top, 122 bottom, 135 left; The Image Works: 71 (Bob Daemmrich), 78 top, 133 left (Zinn Arthur); Thinkstock: back cover; U.S. Fish and Wildlife Service/Mike Bender: 4 top left, 22, 120 (Mike Bender); US Mint: 116 top right, 119 right.

Maps by Map Hero, Inc.